MW00583586

"America has arrived at the headwaters of reason and insanity. We seek direction to remain the country we have always dreamed of and the domain we deserve. The authors of this masterful depiction of truth and fact give credibility to keeping America as the greatest political entity on earth. That means supporting the country and its precious Constitution. *America's Endgame for the 21st Century* serves the country as a first position through valid and patriotic leadership, as written by individuals who have served and are willing to continue serving our great nation. Read the book! In most cases the thoughts contained therein will only be a reminder and renewal of duty, honor, country. For some it will cause alarm and concern and for a few—well, they can't read anyway. Semper Fidelis."

—Jerry Molen, famed Hollywood Producer and
Oscar Award–winner for *Schindler's List*

"My old boss President Ronald Reagan is famous for saying 'Freedom is never more than one generation away from extinction.' Time and again, history has added a facet to this jewel of truth. I pray America is not chiseling its demise today. Thank God for my friends, Generals Vallely and McInerney. Ably assisted by my fellow U.S. Marine veteran, David Goetsch, *America's Endgame for the 21st Century* is a book for our times delineating the peril we face and the way to defeat it. May God help us do what's in this book!"

—LtCol Oliver L. North USMC (Ret.), founder and
CEO of Fidelis Publishing and Fidelis Media,
bestselling author of *Tragic Consequences*

"All doubt has been dispelled about how far America and its people have strayed from the God of the Bible and our nation's founding principles. From a federal government completely out of control to our cities being under siege by unrestrained criminals, hope for a return to peace and prosperity seems lost. Generals Vallely and McInerney with David Goetsch offer solid reason for hope in *America's Endgame for the 21st Century*. While dealing honestly with the darkness cast over our land, they give 'battle plan' strategy for wresting our country from the hands of those who seek its destruction and its return to living under God's grace. Reading and spreading the news about this book can be your way of joining this righteous cause."

—LTG (RET.) Jerry Boykin, EVP Family Research Council,
bestselling author of *Strong and Courageous*

"New threats and new conditions require new assessments. Generals McInerney and Vallely show the way in their new book *America's Endgame for the 21st Century*. McInerney and Vallely provide new analytical tools to address unique threats facing Americans in the twenty-first century. Their groundbreaking analysis provides original insights essential to meet the greatest threat to confront America's experiment in what Abraham Lincoln called government by, for, and of the people. Make no mistake, the founders' experiment in self-government is being tested as Americans have never been tested before by enemies both foreign and domestic. This is a must-read. You will find it an invaluable aid in understanding ruthless new enemies to our constitutional order."

—Col. Andrew P. O'Meara Jr.,
USA (RET) freelance writer and
author of *Liberty Vs. Tyranny*

"Generals Vallely and McInerney are among the most patriotic, most dedicated Americans I have known. It has been my extreme privilege to be associated with them. Along with David Goetsch, they have written an important work that not only needs to be read, but fully absorbed."

—Ray DiLorenzo, member of the board of directors for
The Stand Up America US Foundation, and
managing editor of the Foundation's newsletter

AMERICA'S END GAME

FOR THE 21ST CENTURY

A BLUEPRINT FOR SAVING OUR COUNTRY

LTG THOMAS MCINERNEY, USAF (RET.)
MG PAUL E. VALLELY, USA (RET.)
AND DAVID L. GOETSCH

FIDELIS
PUBLISHING

FIDELIS PUBLISHING

ISBN: 9781956454178
ISBN 9781956454185 (eBook):

America's End Game for the 21st Century
A Blueprint for Saving Our Country

Cover Design by Diana Lawrence
Interior Design by Xcel Graphic
Edited by Amanda Varian

Order discounted books from www.faithfultext.com.

For information about special discounts for bulk purchases, please contact BulkBooks .com, call 1-888-959-5153, or email—cs@bulkbooks.com.

Fidelis Publishing, LLC Sterling, VA • Nashville, TN
fidelispublishing.com
Manufactured in the United States of America
10 9 8 7 6 5 4 3 2 1

From MG Paul E. Vallely

Loving wife and friend forever, Marian (Muffin), Dana (daughter) and Eric Covington, my grandson, Caleb, and my deceased son, Scott Vallely, and my sister, Jewell Willis and family.

From LTG Thomas McInerney

I dedicate this book to:

my father, Col James E. McInerney (WWII and Korean War), my three brothers—Maj Gen James E. McInerney Jr. (Korean War, shot down last Mig 15 in the war; Vietnam War, destroyed the most SAM sites as wild weasel sqn commander; Air Force Cross, three Silver Stars, seven Distinguished Flying Crosses),

Captain Richard N. McInerney (KIA Vietnam as a company commander in 1st Cav Div—Silver Star),

John A. McInerney, twin brother who died seven months after graduation from West Point. All of us were West Point graduates with three of us at West Point simultaneously—a record for a family.

From David L. Goetsch

To my grandsons, Matthew and Henry King, with all my love.

CONTENTS

INTRODUCTION

America's Founders established the United States on a foundation of rock-solid principles, positioning our country to become the strongest and most prosperous bastion of freedom and liberty in the world. These principles include limited republican government of, by, and for the people; private property; a written Constitution; equality of man before God and the law; and individual rights from God, not government. Those rights include freedom of speech, religion, and assembly as well as due process of law.

These founding principles led to the development of a set of values unique to America and Americans. They include individualism, personal responsibility, equal opportunity, looking to the future, learning from the past, achievement, a positive work ethic, efficiency, practicality, informality, upward mobility, success, humanitarianism, and patriotism. The founding principles coupled with these traditional American values set our country apart from all others in ways benefitting not just our citizens but the entire world and made the United States the destination of choice for immigrants worldwide.

Sadly, beginning in the 1960s, Leftist, progressive ideologues rejected everything America stood for and everything that made our country. They initiated a war on God and the United States aimed at replacing our founding principles with Marxism and our traditional values with secular humanism. These Left-wing progressives are determined to destroy America as we know it and rebuild it in their own dystopian, totalitarian image. Yes, changing America forever. To this end, they have taken over the K–12 education system as well as our colleges and universities and have transformed these critical institutions into educational gulags for indoctrinating successive generations of Americans in Leftist orthodoxy. They have driven God out of the schools, government, and the public square. With every step forward these Leftist ideologues have made in advancing their nefarious agenda, America has taken a step backward.

Patriotic Americans are beginning to say, "enough is enough." We wrote *America's End Game for the 21st Century: A Blueprint for Saving Our Country* to provide a gameplan for patriotic Americans who reject the Marxist agenda. Our blueprint for saving America contains seven critical strategies for defeating Leftist ideologues and restoring our country to the principles and values that made it great. These strategies include:

- Achieve an American spiritual revival
- Preserve the Constitution and Bill of Rights
- Reject historical revisionism and refute the big lies of the secular Left
- Preserve capitalism and reject socialism
- Restore patriotism and love of country
- Overcome specific domestic threats to America's end game
- Overcome specific foreign threats to America's end game

We dedicate a full chapter to each strategy and include a comprehensive explanation of what you can do as an American patriot to help implement each strategy. In the epilogue, we paint a picture of what America will look like when patriots like you have done the hard work saving our country from the demonic schemes of the Left. Our prayer is you will join us in this critical battle for America's soul.

Chapter 1

A BLUEPRINT FOR SAVING OUR COUNTRY

The United States of America became the most powerful, prosperous, and free nation ever established because it was founded by stalwart men and women who believed in the principles of self-government, limited government, free enterprise, entrepreneurship, individual liberty, freedom of speech, personal responsibility, constitutional sovereignty, freedom of religion, self-reliance, upward mobility, law and order, unity, initiative, morality, equal opportunity, and a strong military under civilian authority. These values and principles along with the American people who held them made American great.

Unfortunately, these long-standing principles and traditional American values are under attack by Leftist ideologues who reject them outright and are working hard to replace them. America is fast becoming a nation of Socialists, secular humanists, atheists, agnostics, and anarchists who want to tear down the America envisioned by our Founding Fathers, won and sustained by the blood of patriots. They want to replace limited government and self-government with big government, an over-reaching monstrosity controlling every aspect of our daily lives. They want to replace free enterprise, entrepreneurship, and upward mobility with collectivism, individual

1

liberty with group-think and coerced compliance, and freedom of speech with censorship.

Progressive ideologues are trying to replace personal responsibility, self-reliance, and initiative with the victimhood entitlement. They are working hard to transform the Constitution into a meaningless document to be continually revised to accommodate the latest socio-cultural trends. They have made substantial progress in replacing freedom of religion with freedom from religion. Socialists prefer anarchy to law and order as can be seen in their nationwide effort to defund police departments, identity politics and tribalism to E Pluribus Unum, and moral relativism to biblical morality.

When it comes to equal opportunity—which is the law of the land—the Left prefers a nebulous concept known as "equity." Equity is one of those attractive-sounding terms representing an unattractive concept: government coerced equal results regardless of effort, talent, or motivation. Equity is the basis for the absurd everybody-wins-everybody-gets-a-trophy and everybody-makes-the-team fads currently in vogue.

Finally, Leftist ideologues have targeted the military with intentions of using it to force their nefarious social agenda on this critical segment of American society. Instead of focusing on becoming well-trained, well-equipped, well-lead units to protect and defend the United States, military units are being forced by WOKE politicians and compliant, career-protecting officers to focus instead on becoming happy havens for homosexuals and transgendered men and women. They are also focusing their training on convincing troops their white comrades in arms are inherently bigoted and minority troops are perpetual victims.

CONSEQUENCES OF THE LEFT'S WAR ON AMERICA

Actions have consequences. The radical Left's actions over the past sixty years have resulted in tragic consequences for all Americans. The coarsening of the culture by Leftist policies and actions is undeniable. American society is burdened by numerous social problems as a direct result of polices, court decisions, and actions of the Left including hedonism, substance abuse, a vanishing work ethic, rampant abortion, gun violence, mass shootings, mob violence, anarchy, open borders and human trafficking, pornography, censorship, road rage, sideline rage, demise of the traditional family, the politics of personal destruction, and record levels of teen suicides.

Hedonism, Substance Abuse, and the Vanishing Work Ethic

Policies of the Left combined with helicopter parenting are turning young people in America into fragile snowflakes unable to cope with the realities of life in the real world. In the name of "inclusion," the Left has instilled false expectations in young people. Their so-called inclusive practices such as everybody wins, everybody makes the team, and everybody gets a trophy have led young people to expect the world to treat them in this inclusive way. It does not.

Helicopter parents hover over their children doing for them what the children should do themselves, "protecting" them from the consequences of their unruly behavior and giving them everything they need except the two things they need most: responsibility and accountability. When young people raised in this way finally must face the real world without the coerced inclusiveness of the Left and the pampering of their parents, many are—not surprisingly—unable to cope. Therefore, many turn to alcohol and drugs. They are seeking solace from a bottle of liquor or a jar of pills.

America became the greatest nation on earth in large part because of the American people. The American dream used to be upward mobility through hard work, wise decisions, and perseverance. Americans wanted nothing more than the opportunity to build better lives for themselves and their families, and they were willing to work long and hard to achieve this goal. Americans also felt a strong obligation to serve our country and contribute to improving the quality of life in their communities.

Unfortunately, hedonism is undermining the traditional American dream. A hedonist is an individual focused on whatever feels good in the moment with no regard for the long-term consequences. The motto of a hedonist is, "If it feels good do it." This self-indulgent attitude toward life is why America's drug problem has reached epidemic proportions. It is also why American employers have found it so difficult to hire sufficient employees since the beginning of 2021 (the quality thereof is another issue). Leftist politicians in the White House and Congress kept paying people monetary stipends which allowed them to stay home instead of work. Not surprisingly, those with a hedonistic outlook on work and life stayed home.

The new American dream is to get as much as one can while doing as little as possible and to be taken care of by a nanny government. In a hedonistic society the goal is personal pleasure. Sensual self-indulgence has replaced the American work ethic as a central driving force in the lives of a lot of Americans. The work ethic helping make the United States the most productive nation in the world is vanishing. Many Americans today would rather win the lottery and never have to work again than build a better life for themselves through personal initiative and hard work.

Hedonists have the same attitude toward work they have toward life. If it is not fun, do not do it. They have been raised on the fiction that work must be fun, or they are in the wrong job. This, of course, is nonsense. While it is best to like one's job, even the best job in the world is not always fun. If work were always fun, we would call it play and people would do it for free. Work is not always fun, which is why we are paid to do it. This hedonistic attitude toward work is making it difficult for employers to hire and retain the personnel they need to run their businesses. Employee shortages, in turn, are resulting in shortages of essential goods and services, inflated prices, and business closures—facts hurting all Americans.

Rampant Abortion and the Devaluation of Human Life

No public policy is more vociferously guarded by the Left than "legal" abortions. The Left has successfully used the courts to exempt abortion from the biblical proscription against murder found in Exodus 20:13. Leftist ideologues have rewritten the Sixth Commandment to read: *You shall not murder unless you are pregnant with a baby who might pose an inconvenience to you.* What was once a crime in America is now a right celebrated, encouraged, and protected by the Left.

To get around the inconvenient and undeniable truth that abortion amounts to killing innocent babies, the Left engages in one of its favorite but most deplorable practices: semantic subterfuge, which means adopting a palatable name for a deplorable concept. Therefore, the Left refers to abortion as "choice." As a result, 900,000 babies are killed every year in the U.S. in the name of "choice," a fact debasing the value of all human life.

It also robs America of future scientists, Nobel Prize winners, physicians, pastors, military leaders, and other people who could have contributed immeasurably to the betterment of society. Who knows what those 900,000 babies might have become? Devaluing human life has, in turn, led to other social problems including wanton violence and mass shootings.

Gun Violence and Mass Shootings

Who would have ever thought in the United States of America, citizens would settle even minor disputes by pulling out guns and shooting each other? Who would have thought a disgruntled young man would act out his frustration by wiping out classrooms full of little school children or congregations of churches? The gun violence and mass shootings occurring so frequently in America today sound like something out of a B-level horror film, but they are, in fact, real.

Every day in America, gun violence incidents result in the deaths of more than three hundred people or 40,000 per year, facts attributed directly to the Left's refusal to confront its root cause: a society that has so devalued human life that picking up a gun and killing people seems like an acceptable solution to an individual's personal problems. The Left refuses to acknowledge gun violence is a heart problem, not a gun problem.

The Left blames gun violence and mass shootings on guns rather than the people who misuse them and claim gun control is the answer. However, the Left is unable to explain why most legal gun owners never use their guns on other people. Nor can they explain why most people who shoot others, for the most part, obtained their guns illegally. The Left simply cannot admit the obvious: it is the criminal behind the gun, not the gun, that is the problem. Gun violence and mass shootings are what happens in a society that no longer values human life.

Mob Violence and Anarchy

Peaceful protests and demonstrations are constitutionally protected forms of free speech. Such demonstrations have historically taken the form of marches, sit-ins, and boycotts. These forms of peaceful protest were widely used to great effect during the civil rights era. But with the encouragement of the Left, peaceful protests often evolve into riots characterized by looting, arson, and violence. These riots are led by anarchists who use unrest as an excuse to tear down, burn, and loot cities. They have no purpose other than self-aggrandizement and destruction. They act out their frustration with being losers in life by tearing down the world around them.

Rather than take a strong stand against anarchy and mob violence, Leftist governors, mayors, and city leaders often condone and even encourage the riots, siding with the anarchists rather than the police and law-abiding citizens. In 2021, riots led by Black Lives Matter and other anarchist groups sprung up in major cities across the United States. Not only did these riots destroy large sections of these cities, burn out businesses, and injure or kill innocent people, the anarchists who led them demanded these cities defund their police departments. This is like convicts in a state prison demanding all guards be fired and all cell doors and prison gates be left open. What criminal would not want to get rid of the police?

Unbelievably, numerous cities controlled by weak-kneed Leftists agreed with the absurd notion of defunding the police. These cities included Austin, Seattle, New York City, Los Angeles, San Francisco, Oakland, Washington, DC, Baltimore, Portland, Philadelphia, Hartford, Norman, and Salt Lake City. Not surprisingly, as police departments in these cities were trimmed back, violent crime skyrocketed. Consider just one example. As a result of defunding its police department, Portland, Oregon experienced a 500 percent increase in violent crime.

Open Borders and Human Trafficking

When Democrats took control of the White House in 2021, one of their first acts was to throw out all the previous administration's policies protecting America's southern border. Having done this, the new administration announced all comers are welcome. As a result, America's southern border was quickly flooded by millions of illegal immigrants, many of whom are importing diseases and drugs into our country. Among the illegal immigrants coming into America are criminals of the worst kind. Over two-three million illegal border crossers transited the U.S. southern border in 2021 from more than thirty-seven countries.

One of the worst crimes associated with the debacle at our southern border is human trafficking. Many of the immigrants who come to the United States pay human traffickers to get them across the border. Women and young people who get across the border immediately become targets for human traffickers on the American side of the border.

Human trafficking is the commercial trade of human beings through coercion or fraud. Human traffickers treat their victims like a bag of illegal drugs to be sold at the highest possible price. The victims, including young children, are sold into forced labor or sexual slavery. This tragedy is a direct result of the irresponsible policies and practices of Leftist ideologues who are determined to tear down the America that makes immigrants want to come here in the first place. To the Leftist ideologues who threw open our southern border, illegal immigrants are just easily controlled pawns the Left can manipulate for their own nefarious purposes.

Ubiquitous Pornography

Because of the Left's casual attitude toward it, coupled with the unlimited access and anonymity of the internet, pornography has become ubiquitous in America; a plague infecting all levels of American society. As a result, it is destroying families, wrecking marriages, and wreaking havoc on careers, relationships, and even the church.

Thanks to the internet, pornography has become a multi-billion-dollar industry in America rotting the soul of our nation.

As it often does, the Left used the courts to protect and broaden access to pornography. In *Ashcroft v. Free Speech Coalition*, the Left argued that pornographic material produced by consenting adults is protected by the First Amendment.[1] Leftist justices concurred opening the flood gates for anyone with a home computer and camera to produce and distribute any form of pornography except child pornography. There are still severe penalties for producing child pornography, but these penalties have had little effect.

The human traffickers who have been allowed into America at our southern borders have been quick to snatch young girls from among the mobs of illegal immigrants and force them into sexual slavery, using them to produce child pornography distributed over the internet. These human traffickers are already hardened criminals who care nothing about child pornography laws. Many of them have been captured numerous times before by Border Patrol agents and then allowed to return to their countries of origin by Leftist judges.

Cancel Culture and Censorship

Because their policies are indefensible, Leftist ideologues cannot abide dissent. If analyzed carefully and logically, Leftist policies quickly fall apart. Consequently, rather than try to defend their policies, Socialists suppress dissent. Their attitude toward people with differing opinions can be summarized in these words: agree with us or we will destroy you. This attitude has given rise to widespread censorship and the phenomenon known as the *cancel culture*.

Censorship and canceling are how the Left enforces political correctness. Political correctness is political but it is hardly correct. It is a speech and thought control strategy dreamed up by the Left to suppress dissent. The Left, alone, decides what is politically correct. No one else has a say in the matter. If individuals utter a word or statement running counter to Leftist orthodoxy, they are deemed politically incorrect and immediately targeted for suppression.

The Left's original attempts to suppress dissent involved attacking dissenters on the internet and through social media platforms. The concept is known as "flaming." Flaming involves making insulting, profane, and scurrilous comments about an individual on social media or the internet; attacking them continually to make them wary of disagreeing with the Left. Though effective, the Left decided flaming was not sufficiently effective for their purposes. When attacked on social media, people always have the option of simply ignoring the attacks. Then we have the gaslighting of issues and opinions.

Looking for a more effective strategy to scare off dissenters, the Left—working in conjunction with their fellow travelers who own the social media platforms—began censoring people whose views were at odds with Leftist orthodoxy. The most famous example of censorship was when Twitter shutdown President Donald Trump's account. Censoring dissenters amounts to cutting off their access to the world. If they cannot get their messages out, nobody will be able to read them. But even censorship was not enough for the Left, so they escalated their nefarious machinations establishing the cancel culture.

To be cancelled is to be taken off the board, removed from the game, and ruined. The Left attempts to cancel individuals and businesses by organizing boycotts against them, shutting down their social media and internet accounts to deny them access to their audiences, and circulating scurrilous innuendo and outright lies about them. The purpose of the cancel culture is to frighten off dissenters; to make them afraid to speak the truth for fear of retribution. It is the worst attack on freedom of speech in the history of our country. The cancel culture happens in communist China, Cuba, Venezuela, North Korea, and other totalitarian nations, but it should never happen in the United States where freedom of speech is a constitutional right.

Road Rage and Sideline Rage

Two outgrowths of the Left's devaluing of human life that have become scourges on our nation are road rage and sideline rage. In addition to road, we even have airline, bus, and railroad rage. This kind of rage is impatience, anger, or frustration acted out in destructive ways while driving or traveling. Sideline rage is anger acted out in destructive ways, typically at youth sports events such as baseball, football, soccer, and basketball games.

Road rage occurs when one driver inconveniences another by driving too slowly, taking a parking place, sitting through a green light, tailgating, or any number of other perceived offenses. Road rage can take any one of several forms including insults, obscene gestures, brake checking, loud and continual honking of the horn, swerving toward other drivers, and gun violence. Unfortunately, gun violence is becoming a common manifestation of road rage.

Sideline rage typically involves a parent yelling insults at or attacking coaches, umpires, referees, or other parents during youth sports events. Enraged parents have even been known to attack players on the opposing team; players who are just children. People who engage in road rage and sideline rage have clearly lost their perspective. They are willing to shoot, attack, or verbally abuse another human being over something as small as an individual driving slowly or an umpire making a questionable call. Nonetheless, this is the kind of behavior one can expect from people who place no value on human life. The liberals in Congress like Congresswomen Maxine Waters encouraged attacks and rage against any Trump or America First supporter. Yes, attack them anywhere, in public, restaurants, or other gathering places.

Promise of the Traditional Family

To even suggest the traditional family—a man, a woman, and their children—is the natural order of things is to incur the wrath of the Left. A traditional family is based on the sustained marriage of a man and a woman who work together to raise their children. But the Left rejects the concept of the traditional family and is working hard to replace it with single-parent families, homosexual families, and transgender families. Children in grade school are made to read books with titles such as *Why Elliot Has Two Daddies* or *Heather Has Two Mommies*. Add to this the high divorce rate and the number of people who choose to live together without the benefit of marriage and the traditional family in America is in trouble.

If you want to tear down American society as Leftist ideologues do, a good way to begin is by tearing down the most fundamental unit of society: the family. Consider these facts concerning children from traditional two-parent homes versus children from broken or nontraditional homes. Children from traditional two-parent families: 1) are likely to experience fewer social, academic, emotional, or cognitive problems, 2) are more likely to graduate from high school, 3) have a higher employment rate, 4) have a lower out-of-wedlock pregnancy rate, 5) tend to be healthier physically and mentally, and 6) enjoy higher levels of academic achievement.[2]

The family is the foundational building block of American society, more important than even the church in developing successive generations of responsible, contributing citizens. It is where youngsters learn about work, discipline, responsibility, and accountability. It is also where they develop the values directing their choices and decisions throughout life. The Left knows this and, therefore, is willing to do anything to tear down the traditional family. Few things represent a more powerful roadblock to their aspirations than the traditional family.

Politics of Personal Destruction

Nothing demonstrates how mean-spirited and vile the Left can be in advancing its anti-American agenda than the politics of personal destruction. The politics of personal destruction is a contemptible strategy for gaining and retaining political power by destroying the opposition—not defeating but destroying. The principal tactic of Leftists who practice the politics of personal destruction is *character assassination.*

Character assassination involves using innuendo, smearing, false accusations, and outright lies to portray a political opponent as not just unworthy of the office sought, but as an individual of such low character as to be unfit for any office. The worst examples in recent history of how the Left uses character assassination to attack political opponents are the confirmation hearings for Supreme Court Justices Clarence Thomas and Bret Kavanaugh.

Both distinguished jurists were vilified, smeared, disparaged, and denigrated on national television to sway the votes of the Senate Judiciary Committee and derail their confirmation to the Supreme Court. The Left had two goals in mind. First, they wanted to destroy these two Supreme Court candidates to avoid tilting the Court to the Right. Second, they wanted to send a message to future conservatives who might be nominated to the bench, a message that made clear they would pay a price for accepting a presidential nomination.

The worst fear of Leftist ideologues is a Supreme Court willing to overturn the sine qua non of the Left: *Roe v. Wade*, the case "legalizing" abortion. There is no issue more important to the Left than protecting abortion. Fear of the views of Clarence Thomas and Brett Kavanaugh on abortion is why the Left pulled out all the stops to derail their confirmations to the Supreme Court. However, in the process they overplayed their hands revealing to the American people just how low the Left will go to advance its anti-American agenda and to hold onto gains it has made in this regard.

A lot of Americans were appalled and repulsed by the behavior of the Left in their attacks on Thomas and Kavanaugh, but what is even more disgusting than the Left's vile tactics is so many Americans on the Left approved of them. Thomas and Kavanaugh survived the attacks of the Left and were confirmed, but the message to other conservatives who might be appointed in the future was sent loudly and clearly. One can only wonder what effect it has had.

An even more despicable example of the politics of personal destruction can be found in the Left's attacks on Donald Trump. Having failed to prevent the confirmations of two conservative judges, the Left next turned its guns on the president of the United States, Donald Trump. Throughout his presidency and even before he took office, the Left unleased an unrelenting smear campaign against him that continued even after he left office. He was falsely accused of colluding with the Russians to steal the election from Hillary Clinton. Then he was subjected to not just one but two partisan impeachments; one of them after he moved out of the

White House. Even out of office, Trump remained a favorite target of the Left.

The politics of personal destruction and character assassination demonstrate beyond any doubt just how low the Left will go to advance and protect its destructive agenda. This fact, alone, should be sufficient to convince Americans of the need to stand up to the Left, push back against its vile machinations, and reclaim our country for the sake of not just decency but survival.

Teen Suicide

The teen years can be difficult for any young person. Peer pressure, self-image problems, and concerns over body changes complicate the lives of all teenagers. Unfortunately, policies and practices of the Left meant to make life easier for young people just add to the challenge teens face. For example, young people who are raised in an environment of artificial inclusiveness in which everybody makes the team, everybody gets a trophy, and everybody wins eventually learn the world does not work this way. When faced with this reality, some cannot cope, and depression can set in. Except for mental illness, depression is the leading cause of teen suicides, and suicide is the third leading cause of death for young people in America.[3]

The WOKE policies of the Left have transformed America's K–12 public schools into artificial fantasylands condoning, if not inculcating mediocrity, eliminating competition, and focusing on feelings instead of intellectual and character development. Public schools "protect" young people from the realities of the world outside the schoolhouse. In doing this, they leave them unprepared to cope with the realities of that world.

The world does not accept mediocrity, demands competition, and is more concerned with performance than feelings. This reality is often too much for some young people who were raised on artificial inclusiveness and are already struggling with the predictable challenges of the teen years. As a result, depression sets in and, tragically for some, suicide is a better alternative than continuing to struggle. Teen suicides are one more example of how the Left is undermining America's greatest asset: the American people.

WOKENESS Weakened Military

The oath taken by men and women who join any branch of the United States military begins with these words: *"I do solemnly swear (or affirm) that I will support and defend the Constitution of the United States against all enemies foreign and domestic."*[4] This oath, taken at the official swearing-in ceremony, describes the purpose of the U.S. military in a nutshell: to defend the Constitution of the United States against all enemies.

It is not the purpose of the military to help advance the anti-American, anti-Constitution agenda of Leftist ideologues. But the military is being forced by WOKE leaders in the White House, Congress, Department of Defense, and Pentagon, to do just that: advance a Leftist agenda that seeks to tear down the Constitution, not protect it. Officers and enlisted troops are being required to sit through Leftist indoctrination sessions portraying America as an inherently racist nation, white troops as genetically bigoted, and minority troops as hopeless, lifelong victims.

The concept being pushed by the Left and forced on military personnel by weak-kneed, politically-compliant officers is known as *Critical Race Theory (CRT)*. Top officers at the Pentagon, more interested in protecting their pensions than protecting the United States, are going along with Leftist politicians instead of pushing back. In 2021, General Mark Milley, Chairman of the Joint Chiefs of Staff, was promoting CRT which supports racism, runs counter to the Constitution, and undermines the esprit de corps of military personnel. Milley also testified before Congress that he wanted to know and understand "white rage." Of course, as we found out, there was no white rage in the ranks—it was totally made up by this four-star general. The only white rage we have seen in the Armed Forces is from General Milley These progressive generals and admirals were enabled and promoted through the ranks by the likes of Clinton, Obama, and Biden. Yes, politicized senior officers.

At the same time, parents across the nation—black, white, Asian, and Hispanic—were demanding school boards eliminate CRT and pornography from public school curriculums and libraries. These concerned parents, who are interested in education rather than indoctrination for their children, rightly claim CRT is false, divisive, and bad for their children and our country. Parents who are successful in removing CRT from the classrooms of their children are seeing these same children subjected to CRT if they join the military.

When called before a congressional committee to answer for his support of WOKE policies in the military, General Milley tried to defend the teaching of CRT by claiming he read books by Mao tse-Tung but that did not make him a communist. Milley smugly believed he concocted the perfect answer, but unfortunately for him he did not think his answer through well enough. There were holes in Milley's response sensible people could drive a truck through.

For one, he voluntarily read the writings by Mao. He was not forced by the military to read them. Second, he read Mao to learn how the enemy thinks. Military personnel are not volunteering to sit through CRT sessions, they are being forced to. Further, they are not studying CRT to determine how the enemy thinks; they are being taught the enemy is the white comrade in arms sitting right next to them. General Milley read Mao to become a better leader of troops. CRT indoctrination does nothing to improve leadership. In fact, just the opposite. It undermines the ability of officers and NCOs to establish the team spirit and unit cohesion essential to military units. It also undermines the teaching and training of our cadets and midshipmen at the military academies. This distracts from learning vital war tactics and strategies our future officers require to win on the battlefield.

While enemy troops are learning to proficiently use arms and equipment, employ more effective combat tactics, and outperform the American troops on the ground, in the air, and on the sea, our troops are learning to distrust each other based on race. While America's enemies are investing vast sums in continually improving the combat preparedness of their troops, the U.S. military is redirecting badly needed funds to cover the costs of sex-change operations for transgendered troops. In the process, the U.S. military is being weakened as part of a larger Left-wing strategy for taking over our country and turning it into the socialist "paradise" that has failed everywhere it has ever been tried.

AMERICA'S END GAME

With the Left clearly making giant strides in its war on America, what is going to become of our country? The answer to this question is we have a choice. Two paths lay before us. One path—the one preferred by the Left—leads to government control, racial and gender strife, economic stagnation, identity confusion, a culture of WOKEness, a weakened military, removal of God from all aspects of daily life, and the loss of our constitutionally guaranteed freedoms.

The other path leads to a restoration of the vision our Founding Fathers had for the country they created, a vision allowing the United States to become the most powerful, prosperous, and free nation on earth. It's a vision of a "more perfect union" as described in the Preamble to the U.S. Constitution:

> We the people of the United States, in Order to form a more perfect Union, establish justice, insure domestic Tranquility, provide for the common defence, promote the general welfare, and secure the Blessings of Liberty to ourselves and our Posterity, do ordain and establish this Constitution for the United States of America.[5]

Restoring the Founders' vision by recreating that "more perfect union" described in the Preamble to the Constitution is the end game for America for the twenty-first century. Laying out a blueprint for achieving this goal is the purpose of this book. The plan we present herein will allow those of us who still cling to the traditional American values that made America great to save our country. This book is a call to action for all Americans who want to turn our country from its current path—a path leading to destruction—to our former path leading to "a more perfect union."

AMERICA'S FUTURE IS DEPENDENT ON WE THE PEOPLE

After the Bible, Declaration of Independence, and Constitution, the most important documents for Americans are the Federalist Papers. In Federalist 39, James Madison explained a republic is a government which derives all its powers directly or indirectly from the people and is administered by people holding their office at the pleasure of the people for limited period during good behavior.[6]

What Madison wrote in Federalist 39 still applies today. Our republican form of government still derives its powers from the people, but that will change unless we the people stand up, speak out, and fight back against the Leftist ideologues who are trying to destroy our country. If life, liberty, and the pursuit of happiness are to remain defining characteristics of the American way of life, individuals like you and me are going to have to fight for them. What all Americans can do to preserve our liberties and save our country is spelled out in the next section of this chapter. Every patriotic American has a role to play. If we are going to save our country, we will have to look through a *reality prism*, not a *political prism*.

HOW TO ACHIEVE AMERICA'S END GAME: THE BLUEPRINT

The United States of America is 245 years old as of this writing. For most of those years we strived to become the "more perfect union" envisioned by the Founders. Along the way, America fought a great Civil War to put an end to slavery, two world wars to protect freedom-loving nations across the globe from totalitarian tyranny, a cold war with the Soviet Union, and a war on terrorism that continues to this day.

Along the way, we righted lingering wrongs such as the disenfranchisement of black Americans and women. As time went by, America moved closer and closer to being that "more perfect union" described in the Preamble to the Constitution. America has never been perfect, but it has always strived to be. Our country has made mistakes, but it has always strived to learn from them and make the necessary corrections. Therefore, the Left's war on America makes no sense. There is no nation in the world that has worked harder or more consistently to do better and be better.

The Left's attacks on traditional American values and principles are a new phenomenon in the overall history of our country, but in just sixty years Leftist ideologues have made a disturbing amount of "progress." In doing so, they have set America on a path leading to

destruction. Therefore, it is so important for patriots who still want
to see our country be a "more perfect union" envisioned by the
Founders, to stand up, speak out, and join in the battle for America's
soul. Here is what we must come together and do:

- Achieve an American spiritual revival
- Preserve the sovereignty, and integrity of the Constitution and
  Bill of Rights
- Preserve America's true history by rejecting historical revisionism
- Preserve free-market capitalism by rejecting socialism
- Restore patriotism and love of country
- Overcome various domestic threats undermining our achieving
  the end game
- Overcome various foreign threats that could undermine achiev-
  ing the end game

This is the blueprint we recommend for saving America. This
is the blueprint that will allow our country to make continual
progress once again toward becoming "a more perfect union."
This is the blueprint for saving not just our country but the rest
of the free world from despotism, because as goes the United
States, so goes the rest of the free world.

Chapter 2

ACHIEVING AN AMERICAN SPIRITUAL REVIVAL

Electing God-fearing officials who revere the Constitution and hold strongly to traditional American values is a good thing to do, a worthy goal to pursue. However, politicians cannot save our country from the villainous machinations of Leftist ideologues bent on destroying the United States. Why? Because the challenges America faces in the twenty-first century are more basic than politics. America's problems as summarized in chapter 1 are not political; they are spiritual.

As a nation, we have strayed from our spiritual roots and forgotten the biblical principles and values upon which our country was founded. We are like a retired athlete trying to make a comeback. Before competing again, he must first get in shape physically. Before we can save our country from the Left, American patriots must first get in shape spiritually. We need to stop looking to politicians who, no matter how right-minded they may be, still have feet of clay. Instead, we must once again look to God and his Word for salvation, personally, and as a nation.

God knew his children would need spiritual revival. Therefore, he told us in 2 Chronicles 7:14:

"If my people, who are called by my name, will humble themselves and pray and seek my face and turn from their wicked ways, then I will hear from heaven and will forgive their sin and heal their land."

We need God to heal our land. Only he can do it. Presidents cannot, senators cannot, congress men and women cannot, and justices of the Supreme Court cannot. Like you and me, these individuals all have roles to play in saving America from the Left, but only God can restore our nation.

WHAT IS SPIRITUAL REVIVAL AND WHY DO WE NEED IT?

Charles Finney described spiritual revival in these words: "Revival is nothing more or less than a new beginning of obedience to God."[1] A. W. Tozer defined spiritual revival as, "That which changes the moral climate of a community."[2] These are excellent descriptions of the concept. Finney's description shows what individual Americans who want to save our country must do: revive our obedience to God. Tozer's description shows what will happen when we do this: we will change the moral climate of the community and, in turn, our nation.

Because of spiritual neglect, the moral climate in America has gotten progressively worse over the past sixty years or more. We need rejuvenation and restoration. This is what a spiritual revival in America will do. Achieving such a revival is the most essential step we can take toward saving our country. All other elements of the blueprint for America's end game presented in this book depend on achieving this first one: spiritual revival.

We need spiritual revival in America because we need to change the moral climate of our country. That climate is currently characterized by abortion, gun violence, mass shootings, pornography, demise of the traditional family, road rage, substance abuse, the devaluation of human life, and other ugly manifestations of cultural coarseness. Without spiritual revival, these circumstances will just get worse.

While it is easy to blame Leftist ideologues for the declining state of the culture, we need to bear in mind the real culprit is Satan. Leftist ideologues are just his instruments, his evil minions. It is

Satan who is waging war on America and its Christian heritage and values. A hard but undeniable fact is as Christians, we must accept our share of the blame for the current sad state of affairs in our country. In too many cases, we have not fought as hard to preserve God's kingdom as Satan's minions have fought to destroy it. All too often, we let the Left run roughshod over our most cherished beliefs without standing up for those beliefs.

We are now like the retired athlete mentioned earlier who needs to get in top physical shape before making a comeback. We need to get in top spiritual shape before making our own comeback and guiding our country to the path leading away from destruction to restoration. Only when we are wrapped in the armor of God and armed with his Word will we be able to confront, stop, and defeat Satan and the Leftist ideologues he is using to destroy America.

EVIDENCE OF THE NEED FOR SPIRITUAL REVIVAL: A HARD LOOK IN THE MIRROR

We will not be able to do the hard work necessary to save our country from destruction unless we first look in a mirror and admit our own complicity.

This message of personal responsibility is spelled out clearly in Matthew 7:1–5:

> "Judge not, that you be not judged. For with the judgment you pronounce you will be judged, and with the measure you use it will be measured to you. Why do you see the speck that is in your brother's eye, but do not notice the log that is in your own eye? Or how can you say to your brother, 'Let me take the speck out of your eye,' when there is a log in your own eye? You hypocrite, first take the log out of your own eye, and then you will see clearly to take the speck out of your brother's eye."

To help Christian brothers and sisters take that hard look in the mirror, Angela Cleary, writing for Resounding His Love, listed some hard evidence of the need for spiritual revival. According to Cleary, spiritual revival is called for when we:[3]

- Would rather watch television than read the Bible
- Would rather read secular books and magazines than the Bible
- Prefer concerts rather than prayer meetings
- Don't have prayer as a fundamental part of our daily lives
- Make worship a joyless and passionless box-checking exercise
- Know the biblical truth but do not practice it in our lives
- Make little or no effort to reach out to unbelievers
- Put entertainment, sports, and recreation ahead of prayer and Bible study
- Fail to reconcile with fellow believers
- Lack the love of Christ in our marriages
- Ignore sin in the church
- Participate in or just tolerate gossip
- Watch movies or television shows that would not please Christ
- Use prayer to impress others rather than to communicate with God
- Are tolerant of our own sins and those of others
- Turn worship services into entertainment to draw more people in
- Try to fit in with the world rather than calling the world to fit in with God

To these items of evidence, we add one more. Spiritual revival is needed when we use our churches as safe havens from the challenges of life in an increasingly secular nation rather than as "boot camps" to prepare us to confront those challenges. The Great Commission in Matthew 28:18–20 tells us:

"All authority in heaven and on earth has been given to me. Go therefore and make disciples of all nations, baptizing them in the name of the Father and of the Son and of the Holy Spirit, teaching them to observe all that I have commanded you. And behold, I am with you always, to the end of the age."

One of the reasons the Left has made so much headway in its war on America is Christians have, too often, pulled back into their shells and let it happen instead of standing tall for Christ while conducting the Great Commission. Instead of joining the battle for America's soul, too many Christians have sought solace among like-minded believers, used their churches as sanctuaries from the storm raging outside its walls, and spent their time preaching to the choir instead of engaging the enemy: Satan.

Christians who are guilty of any of the sins listed in this section are ill-equipped to play a positive role in taking the fight to Leftist ideologues who want to destroy America. Before we can join the army of God and do the hard work of restoring our country's greatness, we have to fix the man in the mirror.

FIXING THE MAN IN THE MIRROR

When young men and women join the military, they are not just handed a uniform and sent into battle. They must first undergo the crucible of basic training. During this training they are given a unifying purpose: to protect the Constitution of the United States. Then they are taught the basics necessary to conduct this purpose. This same principle applies to Christians who want to help our country undergo spiritual revival as a first step toward putting America on a path leading to salvation, renewal, and restoration.

Before we join the battle for the soul of our nation, we must undergo spiritual basic training. This means we need to establish (or re-establish) our purpose, and then prepare ourselves to achieve that purpose. Our purpose in this endeavor, as in all endeavors, must be putting God at the forefront of our lives and seeking to please him in everything we think, do, and say every day. This means putting aside self-indulgence, self-centeredness, ego, pleasure seeking, fear of confrontation, the desire to fit in with the world, and all the other manifestations of sin that separate us from God.

Once we are committed to serving God instead of self, the next step is to get right with him, so we can carry out this purpose. To do this, begin with 1 John 1:9 where we read: "If we confess our sins, he is faithful and just to forgive us our sins and to cleanse us from all unrighteousness." Fixing the man in the mirror begins and ends with prayer. A warrior in the army of God is first and foremost a prayer warrior.

As you do your part in conducting the various strategies set forth in the blueprint we present in this book, begin by asking God for guidance, perseverance, and the courage to do what must be done. Then ask him to turn the hearts of Leftist ideologues away from their hatred of him and our country and transform them into warriors for Christ and patriotic Americans.

The second step in getting right with God is to arm yourself with his Word. One of the saddest situations to observe is Leftist ideologues able to use the Bible against Christians because they know it better than the Christians who confront them. The Bible is God's sword in your hand when it comes to challenging Satan and his minions. Read it, know it, and take your direction from it. This is the message in Hebrews 4:12:

"For the word of God is living and active, sharper than any two-edged sword, piercing to the division of soul and spirit, of joints and of marrow, and discerning the thoughts and intentions of the heart."

ACHIEVING SPIRITUAL REVIVAL IN AMERICA

Individual Christians considering the enormity of the challenge of achieving spiritual revival in America are likely to think, *What can I do? I'm just one person.* If you are having such doubts while reading this book, we have good news for you. Whether or not America will undergo spiritual revival and the timing of it is in God's hands, not yours. You are not responsible for achieving spiritual revival, but you are responsible for doing your part no matter how small it may seem to you.

In 1955, songwriters Sy Miller and Jill Jackson wrote the song, "Let there be peace on earth and let it begin with me."[4] These lyrics capture the responsibility of individual Christians when it comes to spiritual revival in America. Spiritual revival begins with individual Christians putting God first in their lives and living accordingly. There is a sense in which such a revival is like a major military operation. No matter how large the operation, victory depends on every individual warrior doing his or her part and doing it well. What follows in the remainder of this chapter are ten specific things individual Christians can do to help facilitate spiritual revival in America.

Know and Embrace America's Christian Heritage

In seeking to achieve spiritual revival in America, we are returning to our roots. To do your part in this revival, it is important you know and embrace America's Christian heritage. Our country was founded by Christians who prayed and looked to Scripture for guidance in all their deliberations. For example, of the fifty-six men who signed the Declaration of Independence, at least thirty-two were professing Christians from the following denominations: Episcopalian, Anglican, Congregationalist, Presbyterians, Unitarian, Quaker, and Roman Catholic.[6]

However, to suggest what the historical record clearly shows—America was founded on Christian values and principles—is to invite not just criticism, but ridicule from Leftist ideologues and secular humanists who are trying to tear America down. There is a large and growing element in American society determined to eliminate all evidence of the Christian foundation of American government. This issue of historical revisionism is treated in depth in chapter 4. In this chapter we provide only enough information on this topic to demonstrate America's heritage is decidedly Christian.

One of the cornerstone issues of those who deny the influence of Christianity on America's Founders is the requirement that a wall of separation be maintained between church and state. This is the Left's distorted and false concept of freedom from religion rather than freedom of religion, one of the most pernicious myths ever foisted on the American public.

The wall-of-separation myth had its birth in a misguided Supreme Court decision in 1947 (*Emerson v. Board of Education*) that purposely distorted the wording in a letter written by Thomas Jefferson. The distorted meaning of the letter was used to validate the court's interpretation of the establishment clause of the First Amendment. Jefferson wrote the letter to a Baptist congregation in Danbury, Connecticut, to reassure them there would be no establishment of a state-mandated religion that might result in their denomination being outlawed. In this letter Jefferson wrote of a "wall of separation between church and state" clearly meaning churches were protected by the First Amendment from government interference.[7]

Justice Hugo Black twisted the meaning of Jefferson's letter and used it to justify the Court's decision supporting a wall of separation between church and state. Unlike Jefferson, Justice Black interpreted this to mean government is protected from the influence of churches. Not only did this case represent poor legal scholarship on the part of the Supreme Court, but the decision reached was also an early example of justices violating their constitutional authority by legislating from the bench.

In the first place, to rely on one paragraph from one letter written by one individual to justify a decision of this magnitude was not just questionable, it was irresponsible. When you consider there are reams of founding documents easily accessible to anyone conducting research on this subject, it is difficult to understand why one paragraph from one letter written by one Founder could carry so much weight. Difficult, that is, unless the justices in question made their decisions about the establishment clause of the First Amendment based on personal bias rather than legal scholarship. The justices in the majority in *Everson v. Board of Education* appear to have been looking for a way to validate a decision they already made, and Jefferson's letter could be twisted to suit their purpose. This kind of perfidy has become widespread practice among those who deny the influence of Christianity on the Founders and, in turn, American government.

While it is true our Founders opposed false divinity, the divinity they opposed was not the God of Holy Scripture but that of kings and queens, the self-proclaimed divinity of European royalty. America's Founders believed people could be judged superior to one another only on the basis of merit, not birth; a sentiment reflected in the Declaration of Independence which begins:

> We hold these truths to be self-evident that all men are cre-
> ated equal; that they are endowed by their Creator with
> certain unalienable rights . . .[8]

In other words, the rights of the people—including religious liberty—come from God not monarchs.

By the time the Founders drafted the Constitution, Europe had a long history of monarchs claiming to be rulers by divine right and then using their power to make their religion the only acceptable and allowable religion. The Founders universally rejected the divinity of human monarchs and set about establishing a country in which the people being ruled would choose their rulers as well as their religions.

Further, the Founders expected those who governed as well as those who were governed to be guided by the values and principles set forth in Holy Scripture. Without understanding how European monarchs persecuted subjects who subscribed to any but the state-approved religion, it is difficult to understand how important pre-venting the government from undermining freedom of religion was to the Founders. But even a cursory study of the founding docu-ments validates this contention.

The religion clause of the First Amendment reads as follows:

> Congress shall make no law respecting an establishment of
> religion or prohibiting the free exercise thereof . . . [9]

Advocates of a wall-of-separation emphasize the establishment clause of the First Amendment while conveniently ignoring the free-exercise clause. Over time, this emphasis has transformed the concept of freedom OF religion into freedom FROM religion, or at least freedom from the Christian religion.

This was never the intention of the Founders. The Founders universally encouraged religion and valued its beneficial effects on human thinking and behavior. What they opposed was not religion, but state-mandated religion in which the only denomination allowed was the one prescribed by those who held the reins of power. Guard-ing against this type of state-sponsored coercion was the subject of Thomas Jefferson's letter to the Danbury Baptists, misconstrued by the Supreme Court in its infamous "separation of church and state" decision in 1947.

A more thorough study of the founding documents would have shown the Supreme Court justices that the brave men and women who risked everything to establish the United States of America had no intention of erecting a wall of separation to keep the church out of the state. Quite the contrary, the establishment clause of the First Amendment—one of the most grossly misinterpreted clauses in the Constitution—was intended to protect citizens from a state-sponsored church that could tax them for support while banning attendance at any other church; the very situation the Pilgrims came to America to escape.

It is worth noting at this point that Americans in the late 1700s were overwhelmingly Christian. Ninety-nine percent of them were either Protestant or Catholic. Having made this point, when we state America rests on a Christian foundation, we do not claim our country was founded as a theocracy or that only Christians can be Americans. Rather, we state what is obvious from the historical record: our Founders were guided by the moral values of Holy Scripture in their deliberations, beliefs, and subsequent actions just as all Americans should be as we engage in the political process. The Christianity of the Founders was a powerful force in shaping their views and actions.

The Founders believed people should be free to practice their religion or not without government interference or coercion. They envisioned a nation in which religion was an issue between God and the people, not government and the people. Having said this, it is important to understand peer pressure in favor of the Christian religion was much stronger in the days of the Founders, as can be seen in the historical record. In the days of the Founders, Christian values were a given, not something debated in the public square or denied by secular humanists pushing an anti-Christian agenda.

Seek to Please God, Not Man

The spiritual revival needed in America begins with believers seeking to please God, not man; seeking to fit in with God, not the world; and reaching out to unbelievers and showing them why

ACHIEVING AN AMERICAN SPIRITUAL REVIVAL

God's way is the better way. Because of what happened in the garden of Eden, we are a fallen people living in a fallen world. Hence, our human tendency is to seek the approval of the world, not God. We seek recognition and validation from people rather than God.

This approach to life is unfortunate because the approval of the world is fleeting and unfulfilling. This is the message in Ecclesiastes 1:2 where we read, "Vanity of vanities, says the Preacher, vanity of vanities! All is vanity." People tend to interpret the term "vanity" from Ecclesiastes as excessive pride, but a more accurate reading of the term, as used in this passage of Scripture, is "pointlessness." The approval of the world is pointless because it feeds the ego, not the soul. Only God's approval can feed the soul.

To make matters worse, worldly approval is addictive. Once you become hooked on it, worldly approval shapes your self-image, feeds your ego, makes you prideful, and turns you away from God. The more worldly approval you receive, the more you want. Eventually you become like the drug addict who cannot function without ever-increasing amounts of the poison. Worse yet, worldly approval is fleeting. In the eyes of the world, you can be a hero today and forgotten tomorrow.

Seeking the approval of God rather than the world may turn out to be one of the most difficult things you ever try to do. Worldly approval, like most temptations, can be powerfully appealing. It is like the aroma of coffee and donuts wafting from a bakery early in the morning or the allure of an ice-cold drink on a swelteringly summer day. It appeals to something deep inside us. Worldly approval tugs at the very core of our human frailties. Among other things, it appeals to our fears, ambition, ego, need to fit in, desire for validation, and preference for immediacy. These human desires are powerful, but trying to satisfy them instead of seeking to honor God leads to nothing but a life of pointlessness and frustration.

What does it mean in practical terms to please God instead of pleasing the world? How does one go about pleasing God instead of man? What follows are specific things you can do to please God:

1. Acknowledge God as the author of your achievements and blessings.

2. Heed the Greatest Commandment in all aspects of your life.
3. Pray for God's help.
4. Seek guidance in Scripture.
5. Seek the wise counsel of fellow believers.

Whenever you find yourself wanting to fit in with the world to the detriment of fitting in with God, go through each of these five steps. We will never be able to save our country from the machinations of the Left until we commit to pleasing God in all we do.

Speak the Truth in Love to Unbelievers—Engage, Do Not Condemn

One of the most difficult challenges we face as Christians is establishing, building, and maintaining relationships with unbelievers, particularly those who are determined to destroy our country. There are two keys to establishing and maintaining positive relationships with unbelievers; engage but do not condemn and speak the truth in love. This is the message in Ephesians 4:15:

> "Rather, speaking the truth in love, we are to grow up in every way into him who is the head, into Christ."

When interacting with Leftist ideologues, you are not likely to win them to Christ by beating them over the head with the Bible and damning them to hell.

On the other hand, do not make the mistake of soft-soaping what you have to say just to avoid conflict. When you interact with Leftist ideologues, secular humanists, and others who reject God, speak the truth from Scripture, but do so in a spirit of Christian love. Never forget your goal in engaging unbelievers is to win them for Christ, not to win the argument. Speaking the truth in love and engaging without condemning will help you disagree without being disagreeable, an important skill for those who want to engage unbelievers.

Relationships are built on trust and mutual respect. This can make engaging unbelievers a challenge. It can be difficult to trust or respect people who reject your beliefs. Therefore, some

Christians choose to limit their relationships to fellow believers. Although this approach may be more comfortable than engaging unbelievers, it is at odds with the teachings of Scripture. We cannot do our part to conduct the Great Commission (Matt. 28:19) unless we are willing to engage unbelievers and invest the time and effort necessary to build positive relationships with them.

The most important ingredient in building good relationships is honesty. Speaking the truth in love to people who may not want to hear it means being honest with them, even when your honesty may hurt. Of course, it is important to be tactful when speaking the truth to unbelievers. Think of tact as making your point without making an enemy or driving in the nail without breaking the board. Berating Leftist ideologues will not help you establish mutually respectful relationships, nor will it lead them to Christ. Remember, these folks are blinded by our mutual enemy, Satan.

On the other hand, you must be honest with unbelievers. When their words or actions fly in the face of God's Word, you have a biblical obligation to speak up. Scripture is replete with admonitions to be honest, not the least of which is the Ninth Commandment (Exod. 20:16). If you are going to influence unbelievers for good, they must trust you. Those you hope to influence must know they can count on you to tell them the truth and deal forthrightly with them on all subjects even when they do not like the message.

Scripture speaks to honesty in Proverbs 11:1 where we are told a "false balance" is an "abomination to the Lord." The broader meaning of this verse is God expects us to be honest with other people, to speak the truth; but he expects us to do this out of love not condemnation. When Leftist ideologues know you are confronting their rejection of God out of love rather than condemnation, they will be more likely to hear the message you are trying to convey—not at first, but over time.

When engaging unbelievers, remember people do not have to endorse your beliefs to respect them, nor do they have to share your beliefs to trust you. Further, just because people act in sinful ways does not necessarily mean they reject your Christian values. People often shun Christianity not because they reject its values but because they do not want to live by its precepts. Most people respect honesty, trustworthiness, patience, kindness, and other Christian values even if they fall short in these areas themselves.

To build relationships with unbelievers that will help you conduct the Great Commission, be honest with them and build trust. Speak the truth to them but do it in love. When it comes to accepting the gospel, unbelievers must first have eyes to see, ears to hear, and hearts to understand (Deut. 29:4). The trusting, truthful, caring relationships you establish with unbelievers might open their eyes, ears, and hearts to God's Spirit so they can see, hear, and understand the gospel. When this happens, they will become a new member of the army of God rather than a rejector of him bent on destroying America.

Show God's Love to the Unlovable

It is hard to imagine anyone less lovable than a Leftist ideologue bent on rejecting God and tearing down America. Therefore 1 Corinthians 13 is so crucial to the spiritual revival needed in America. It presents Christians with one of the most difficult challenges we will ever face: showing the unlovable the love of God. First Corinthians is about showing biblical love to everyone, which is hard enough by itself, but when you consider "everyone" includes those who do not seem to deserve your love the challenge becomes even more difficult.

As human beings, it is tempting to associate only with people whose worldviews agree with ours. This is natural. There is comfort in common ground. However, as Christians, you and I are called to interact positively with people of all worldviews, believers, and unbelievers. Associating positively with unbelievers does not require you to condone inappropriate behavior, nor does it mean compromising your faith to have a good relationship with them. Rather, it means interacting in ways that reflect the image of Christ rather than segregating yourself from those who do not know him.

We are children of God the Father; there should be a family resemblance. As children of God, we should reflect the image of Christ in all we do. This is best done by setting a Christlike example. The Bible is replete with guidance concerning the importance of setting a good example. In fact, James 4:17 makes clear that knowing the right thing to do but failing to do it is a sin. Therefore, not only is setting a Christlike example the right thing to do, failing to set such an example is a sin.

To learn how to love the unlovable, read 1 Corinthians 13. This chapter in Scripture is God's classic exposition about love. Consequently, when trying to set a Christlike example for unbelievers as well as fellow believers, 1 Corinthians 13 is an essential reference. The type of love described in 1 Corinthians 13 has nine characteristics, all of which have specific application for showing Christ's love to the unlovable:

1. Patient
2. Kind
3. Not jealous or envious
4. Not boastful
5. Not arrogant
6. Becoming in its actions
7. Seeks the good of others rather than seeking its own
8. Not provoked
9. Keeps no records of wrong done by others.

Setting an example of these characteristics will be difficult in the best circumstances. However, it will be especially difficult when engaging wolves who would not think twice about devouring you. However, the closer you come to incorporating the love of 1 Corinthians 13 into the example you set for unbelievers, the more effective you will be. Even more important, the closer you come to incorporating the love of 1 Corinthians 13 into your example, the more pleasing you will be to God.

Lessons abound in 1 Corinthians 13 for those of us who are called to set a Christlike example for Leftist ideologues and other unbelievers. One of the most important of these lessons comes in verse 1. This verse tells us no matter how honestly or articulately we speak, if our words are not spoken in love, they are like a "noisy gong" or a "clanging cymbal." When you disagree with someone, doing so in a considerate, respectful manner without becoming

disagreeable will provide a powerful example of Christian forbearance for them. It will, no doubt, also be a welcome change for
people who are accustomed to being attacked by those who disagree
with them. The number of people who have learned to disagree
without being disagreeable is, unfortunately, small.

In committing to model Christ in ways exemplifying 1 Corinthians 13, you are agreeing to demonstrate a love that serves others
before self. But how does one translate this kind of love into practical action? The following list contains examples of specific things
you can do to translate 1 Corinthians 13 into practical action:

- Help others.
- Listen attentively to others when they need to talk.
- Be willing to forgive and ask for forgiveness.
- Support others who are right even when doing so is difficult.
- Refuse to mistreat others no matter how unworthy they may
  seem.
- Refuse to encourage others to do wrong.
- Refuse to take pleasure in the misfortune of others.
- Refuse to embarrass others by saying or doing things that make
  them look or feel foolish.
- Refuse to abuse others emotionally or physically.
- Refuse to wish misfortune on others.

As you can see from these practical, everyday tactics, being a
1 Corinthians 13 Christian will never be easy. The most difficult
part, of course, is to be loving, patient, and kind to those who do
not reciprocate. However, while it is true exemplifying 1 Corinthians 13 is no guarantee of reciprocal treatment, it is also true
it is harder for people to treat you poorly when you treat them
well. Patience and long-suffering will no doubt be necessary as
you struggle to set a Christlike example day after day. When you
become frustrated with setting a good example for people who do
not reciprocate, think of what is written in Galatians 6:9 where
we are told to avoid becoming weary in doing good because our
reward will come in God's enjoyable time if we persevere.

A caveat is in order here. Setting a 1 Corinthians 13 example does not require you to meekly allow people to run over or abuse you. As Christians, we are not called to be helpless doormats. Rather, setting a Christlike example means showing others the image of Christ in how you respond when they treat you badly. In disagreements over moral issues, those who fight fire with fire just make a bigger fire. As Christians, we are to confront and reject sin in any setting. But how we go about this is important.

When responding to those who treat you badly, remember the admonition in Proverbs 25:21–22 to feed our enemy if he is hungry and give him water if he is thirsty. This verse reminds us that doing these things will "heap burning coals" on the head of our adversary on one hand and bring us rewards from God on the other.

Be a Missionary in Hostile Territory—Serve Where God Plants You

Christians can be forgiven for thinking they are living in hostile territory in the America of today. God is no longer welcome in schools, government, the workplace, or the public square. Because of this, America's spiritual revival depends on individual Christians committing to being missionaries in their own country. We need to serve as missionaries wherever God has planted us.

Being an at-home missionary begins by heeding the message in 1 Corinthians 11:1 where Christ tells us to be imitators of him. This can be a difficult challenge when doing so subjects you to pressure, rejection, and even threats, but do not despair. Whether in school, on the job, or in any other environment, you can be a faithful witness for Christ. The key to doing so is found in Christ's own words where he tells us be imitators of him.

You do not have to hand out tracts or verbally evangelize to spread the gospel, though those tactics can work. In some settings these approaches are not likely to be effective. But do not despair; there is an approach to witnessing for Christ that is not just appropriate in any setting, it is also effective. No matter what setting you find yourself in, you can show others the face of Christ by how you do your work, treat other people, make decisions, respond to challenges, handle grief, face adversity, and behave in emergencies. In other words, by setting a Christlike example for the people you interact with.

For believers, appropriate responses to anti-Christian pressure, rejection, and even persecution are those exemplified in Scripture. They are responses personifying what is written in Titus 2:7. In this verse, we are told to show ourselves to be models of "good works." This verse also admonishes us to demonstrate "integrity" and "dignity" in our teaching. Remember, you teach best by example. You can set a Christlike example in even the most hostile territory because doing so means being honest, loving, caring, dependable, conscientious, and industrious. Even the most hardened rejectors of Christ appreciate interacting with people who personify these Christlike traits.

We fully understand how difficult it can be to respond to temptation, rejection, and pressure in ways consistent with the teaching of Christ. Secular humanism, moral relativism, and political correctness permeate all aspects of American society generating ever-increasing levels of anti-Christian bias. Swimming upstream against the current of anti-Christian bias is not easy. We do not want to understate this fact. Therefore, Christians who are trying to be at-home missionaries should heed Christ's instructions to his apostles before sending them out to spread the gospel. In Matthew 10:16 Christ told the apostles they were going to be like sheep in the midst of wolves. Therefore, they would need to be both wise and innocent. This is good advice for you too.

Live Your Faith—Do Not Hide It

To avoid conflict and rejection or to fit in, some Christians resort to hiding their faith; they go along to get along. Christians who hide or downplay their faith do so to avoid letting it become an issue with unbelievers. They do not want to rock the boat. America will never undergo a spiritual revival if Christians hide their faith. To do your part in bringing about a spiritual revival, do not hide your faith—live it.

Christians who hide their faith, regardless the reasons, are ignoring the lesson in Matthew 5:14–16. In these verses, we are told to let our lights shine in ways allowing others to see our good works and how we use those good works to glorify God. As Christians, we are to shine our lights, not hide them.

Before continuing, a caveat is in order. It is not our intention to belittle fellow believers who feel compelled to hide their faith in favor of social acceptance, job security, career advancement, or other appropriate goals. We understand how difficult it can be to feel left out socially, at work, or in any other setting. No one should be criticized for wanting to have friends or fit in at school or work. But how we go about winning friends or fitting in does matter.

As Christians, we can have friends without compromising our faith. The keys to doing this are: 1) heed the admonition in Matthew 10:16 to be both wise and innocent, and 2) remember our fervent desire must be to please God, not man. Live your faith. Let it shine through in everything you think, do, and say every day. Never put on an act. You do not have to act because no matter where you are or what you are doing, be who you are: a child of God. You never know the effect your living example will have on unbelievers.

Love Your Neighbor as Yourself

In Matthew 22:39 Christ is evaluated by a Pharisee lawyer. To trip him up, the lawyer asks Jesus to reveal which is the greatest commandment. But Christ turns the tables on the Pharisee by stating what has come to be known as the "Great Commandment" (Matt. 22:37–39):

> "You shall love the Lord your God with all your heart and with all your soul and with all your mind. This is the great and first commandment. And a second is like it: You shall love your neighbor as yourself."

With these words, Jesus not only made a self-important Pharisee look foolish, but he also gave you and me our marching orders for how we are supposed to live.

But what does it mean to love our neighbors as ourselves? How do we translate the second part of the Great Commandment into action? What follows are ten specific things you can do to demonstrate Christian love toward your neighbors, including those who are Leftist ideologues who want to destroy our country. Doing these things will require you to replace your natural human inclination toward self-centeredness with an attitude of service over self. You can do this by repeating the following ten tactics over and over until they become your new normal:

1. Practice kindness and gentleness.
2. Practice patience and forbearance.
3. Practice contentment and peace.
4. Practice humility and modesty.
5. Practice faithfulness and consideration.
6. Practice encouragement and goodness.
7. Practice selflessness and charity.
8. Practice self-control and imperturbability.
9. Practice graciousness and forgiveness.
10. Practice honesty and integrity.

Consistently demonstrating love for your neighbors by putting service before self will never be easy, and the challenge becomes even more difficult when trying to show the love of Christ to people who do not respond in kind. People who are unlovable and unappreciative of your efforts are going to cause you no end of frustration and doubt. Count on it. It is always easier to treat people well when they are appreciative and agreeable. Unfortunately, people are often just the opposite. The Leftist ideologues who reject God and want to destroy America are not likely to be appreciative or agreeable.

You may find it difficult to love neighbors who do not seem to deserve your love. If this happens to you, remember the Lord loves you and me, even when we do not deserve it. In fact, it has been said you have not loved in the Christian sense until you have loved the unlovable. Christ's unfailing love for us is an example of loving the unlovable. Walking in the footsteps of Christ and emulating his example will never be easy for sinners living in a fallen world. But then, something as earth-shakingly profound as spiritual revival is not supposed to be easy.

With this said, the ten tactics recommended above are designed to help you replace what comes naturally to sinners with an innovative approach to life; an approach that will bring you closer to God in your daily walk. This approach is best described as service over self. These tactics will help you practice doing what Christ expects of you until the challenging work of loving your neighbor becomes your normal way of doing things. When this happens, not only will the recipients of your love benefit, but you will and so will America.

Learn to Forgive Even When It Is Difficult

Christ died on the cross so you and I could be forgiven our sins. This was the most powerful demonstration of unmerited grace the world has ever known. Because Christ is our example in all things, forgiveness must be a fundamental aspect of our daily walk. It is especially important when engaging Leftist ideologues, secular humanists, and others who reject God and want to tear down our country. We cannot reflect the image of Christ unless we are prepared to forgive their transgressions, as Christ forgives ours. Yet for many people, forgiveness is easier to apply in theory than in practice. When it comes to sharing the fruit of the Spirit, forgiveness is often left hanging on the tree.

People who reject God and hate America are going to say and do things that anger, frustrate, and discourage you. Count on it. The worst thing you can do in this type of situation is respond in anger and become like the haters. Engaging Leftist ideologues and secular humanists can be like engaging in a mud fight without a raincoat. You are going to get some mud on you. The key to whether the mud sticks is your willingness to forgive. When you find yourself unable to forgive those who reject God and hate our country, remember Christ's dying words on the cross, "Father, forgive them, for they know not what they do" (Luke 23:34). Like those who killed Jesus Christ, those who are trying to kill America know not what they do.

One of the reasons people struggle with forgiveness is they do not understand what it means. Forgiveness in this context involves consciously putting aside feelings of resentment even though the offending individuals are, in fact, guilty or at least you think they are. When the Lord forgives, it means he no longer holds our transgression against us. It does not mean we did not transgress. The kind of forgiveness we advocate here is not the kind that absolves the sinner, rather it releases us from the anger and resentment their offense causes. Keep in mind, Christ died for these people who hate him and us and if they don't turn, they will spend eternity in torment we can't even imagine.

Where people sometimes get off track in their thinking when it comes to forgiveness is in viewing it as exoneration. They think by forgiving they are saying their offenders are innocent. This view of forgiveness is not just misguided, it is wrong. Forgiving offenders is different from telling them, "You are not guilty." If the individuals in question were not guilty, they would not need forgiveness. Never forget the Lord forgives us even though we are guilty, not because we are innocent. However, this level of forgiveness requires repentance, admission of and turning from sin.

Know How to Respond to Repeated Rejection

Secular humanism, moral relativism, and political correctness are becoming the norm in contemporary society, a fact making life difficult for Christians. Therefore, we are seeing increasingly anti-Christian bias in our daily lives. A growing number of people claim they are offended by the mere mention of Christianity. Consequently, as Christians attempting to engage Leftist ideologues, secular humanists, and others who reject God, we face the daily challenge of remaining faithful to our beliefs when interacting with people who repeatedly and often stridently reject them.

As a believer in today's increasingly anti-Christian culture, your faith is going to be challenged. Count on it so you won't be surprised when it happens. Christ warned us of this in John 15:18. Understand the devil is a predator who never stops hunting, and you, like all Christians, are his prey (1 Pet. 5:8). When your faith is challenged, do not despair. Instead, remember this: suffering in the short run for your beliefs is better than suffering overall for compromising them. Persevering in the faith is always the right decision when your Christian beliefs are attacked.

Consistently living your faith is almost guaranteed to cause you problems from time to time. In fact, the closer you walk with the Lord the more resistance you are likely to face in today's increasingly anti-Christian environment. Nevertheless, maintaining your faith when others reject it is always the right choice. Consider what is written in Hebrews 12:3. This verse reminds us Christ suffered for us, and there has never been a time when Christians did not suffer for their faith. Consequently, we should not grow weary when we must suffer. Suffering for our faith is part of being a Christian.

How should we respond when faced with repeated rejection from unbelievers we are trying to engage? We recommend a five step model. The model summarizes the steps Christians should take when confronted by repeated rejections and challenges to our faith.

Step 1: Avoid responding out of anger, fear, or frustration.

It is important to stand firm in your faith when others attack it, but it is equally important to respond in a Christlike manner. On one hand, you are not called to be a doormat for people who hate Christ, but on the other hand, you do not want to become like them by responding the same way. Recall when Satan tempted Christ in the wilderness. Jesus responded with the authority of his Father rather than out of anger, fear, or frustration. Christ is our example. Thus, our responses to rejection and even persecution should be Christlike.

Responses driven by anger, fear, or frustration are not likely to be Christlike responses. Consequently, when you want to respond in a way that would reflect poorly on Christ, take a deep breath, and do not respond at all, at least not in the moment. Follow the guidance provided in Psalm 37:8 where we are told to refrain from anger because it leads only to evil. Instead of responding out of anger, fear, or frustration, step back and give yourself time to complete the remaining steps in this model.

Step 2: Pray for guidance.

Never deal with faith-related trials without enlisting the help of God. In 1 Thessalonians 5:17, Paul says we are to pray constantly. Remember, no matter how helpless you may feel, all things are possible with God. The Holy Spirit is right there with you. He will be there at your side as you confront those who reject him. Seek God's guidance through prayer. Remember, Proverbs 20:24 makes clear we cannot understand even our own way without the help of the Lord. This is another reason we should heed Paul's admonition to pray constantly.

When you pray, ask Christ what he would have you do. Then listen. Never make the mistake of trying to go it alone or of thinking you are self-sufficient when confronted by Satan and his minions. Without the help of God, Satan will win, and you will lose. Satan's power compared to yours is that of an elephant trampling a flea. But compared to Christ, Satan is powerless. With God's help, you will win, and Satan will lose.

Step 3: Seek guidance in Scripture.

Every challenge you will ever face is spoken to in the Bible. Holy Scripture provides God's guidance concerning how we should live, interact with others, face dilemmas, and solve problems, as well as how we should honor him in how we do these things. Consequently, when facing faith-related trials, it is both wise and innocent to consult Scripture before action of any kind (Matt. 10:16). A word of caution is appropriate at this point. When you consult Scripture, do so to determine what God would have you do in each situation, not to validate what you have already decided to do. Using the Bible to rationalize decisions you have already made is neither wise nor innocent. The Bible does not always tell you what you want to hear, but it does tell you what you need to hear.

Step 4: Seek the wise counsel of godly men and women.

One of the many benefits of being a Christian with a church family is you have brothers and sisters in Christ to help you face challenges to your faith. A fellow Christian might have already faced the challenge confronting you now. That individual's experiences—good and bad—might help you formulate your response. Asking for help is not a sign of weakness; it is a sign of wisdom.

The Bible is clear in its admonition that Christians are to seek the counsel of godly men and women. Proverbs 12:15 makes clear seeking wise counsel is the smart thing to do. Seeking wise counsel can involve talking to your pastor, a Christian counselor, fellow believers, or all of these. Never skip this step. God often does his work through individual Christians. Hence, he might use one of your brothers or sisters in Christ to help you deal with the challenge you are facing.

Step 5: Translate scriptural guidance and wise counsel into practical action.

We have stressed that your best guidance for confronting faith related challenges will come from prayer, reading the Bible, and seeking the wise counsel of Christian brothers and sisters. The answers you need are available, but it is not enough to pray, read Scripture, and seek wise counsel. You cannot stop there. Rather, you must translate what you learn from these exercises into practical action.

Philippians 4:9 makes clear what we have learned and heard from God is to be put into action. How to put scriptural guidance and wise counsel into action will not always be obvious. Consequently, it is important to remember the message in Matthew 10:16, be wise and innocent when translating scriptural guidance and wise counsel into practical action. Be tactful, kind, and respectful, but do not deviate from the path God has set for you.

Walk Worthy of Your Calling Every Day

It is often said pastors are "called to preach." We have even heard people who work in secular professions say, "This position is more than a job—it's a calling." A calling is a powerful inner desire provided by God for you to pursue a certain course of action. A calling, in the current context, is more than just a personal desire to be or do something. It is a desire etched on your heart by God to do your part in helping bring about spiritual revival in America as the first and most crucial step toward saving our country.

What follows are specific things you can do to walk worthy of your calling to be a soldier in the army of God dedicated to saving America from the nefarious machinations of Leftist ideologues, secular humanists, and others who eject God and want to destroy our country:

- Seek first to please God in all aspects of your life.
- Show others Christian character, love, kindness, gentleness, and patience.
- Demonstrate unity of the Spirit in the bond of peace.
- Set an example of excellence by exemplifying the Christian work ethic.
- Balance faith, family, and work.
- Be grateful for your blessings and acknowledge their source.
- Show others respect.
- Be humble and gentle.
- Sacrifice for your neighbor—be helpful and giving.
- Forgive those who seek forgiveness.
- Persevere in the faith when life becomes difficult.

By doing these things, you can walk worthy of your calling and do your part to bring about spiritual revival and save America. When this happens, at the name of Jesus every knee shall bow (Phil. 2:10) and when that happens, America will be saved.

CHAPTER 3

PRESERVING THE CONSTITUTION AND BILL OF RIGHTS

The United States of America is more than just a country on a map, it is an idea; an idea captured eloquently by Thomas Jefferson in the Declaration of Independence when he wrote: "We hold these truths to be self-evident, that all men are created equal, that they are endowed by their creator with certain unalienable Rights, that among these are Life, Liberty, and the pursuit of Happiness. That to secure these rights, Governments are instituted among Men, deriving their just powers from the consent of the governed . . ."[1] Precisely how the government of the United States is to be "constituted among men" and how the government is to derive its "just powers from the consent of the governed" is set forth in the Constitution.

The Constitution is under attack by Leftist ideologues who are trying to change it in ways so drastic that the government President Abraham Lincoln said should be "of the people, by the people, and for the people"[2] is being transformed into a government of the state, by the state, and for the state. If Americans do not do what is necessary to reverse this trend and restore the Constitution to the original intent of the Founders, the great experiment described by Thomas Jefferson will fail and the idea of America will die.

A BRIEF REVIEW OF THE CONSTITUTION

It is a sad fact that many Americans have never read the U.S. Constitution. This must change. If we are going to preserve the Constitution and Bill of Rights as part of the blueprint for saving America, we must know what these documents say. The information contained in this chapter is the minimum all Americans should know about the Constitution.

The Constitution is one of the most significant documents ever written. In fact, for Americans the three most important documents in existence are the Holy Bible, Declaration of Independence, and Constitution. All three are under attack from the Left. All three must be preserved if our country is to be saved and restored.

Known as the father of the Constitution, James Madison kept a journal of the debates occurring during the development of the original document. From Madison's notes we can learn much about the men who developed the document. Writing about the framers of the Constitution, historians Edward S. Greenburg and Benjamin I. Page noted, ". . . the delegates were conversant with the great works of Western philosophy and political science; with great facility and frequency, they quoted Aristotle, Plato, Locke, Montesquieu, and scores of other thinkers. They were also surprisingly young, averaging barely over 40 years of age. Finally, these delegates, who became the framers of the U.S. Constitution, had broad experience in American politics—most had served in their state legislatures—and many were veterans of the Revolutionary War."[3]

If the Declaration of Independence represents America's vision, the Constitution is the game plan for realizing that vision. Key principles in the Constitution as set forth by the Founders are:

- *Republican Form of Government.* A form of government based on consent of the governed, it includes guards against pure majoritarian democracy while also protecting against all forms of government tyranny. With republicanism, public policies are made by representatives elected by the people rather than directly by the people, as would be the case with pure democracy. Federalist Papers numbers 10 and 51 written by James Madison, describe the republican form of government, America's particular form of republican government, and the rationale for it in greater detail.

- *Selection of Government Leaders by Election.* The people's representatives—congresspeople, senators, and the president—who make public policy are elected by the people. Of course, in the case of the president there is the electoral college, but the people still elect the president indirectly. This approach ensures there is popular consent of the governed and participation by the governed while also protecting against the possibility of a tyrannical government of the few ruling the many.

- *Limited Federalism.* The Constitution did away with the loose confederation of states established by its predecessor, the Articles of Confederation. In its place was established a federal system, but a limited federal system. In this system, some powers are given to the federal government, some are forbidden to the states, some are shared by the state and federal governments, and the rest are left to the states. Article VI, Section 2, of the Constitution, known as the "Supremacy Clause," describes the federal system it established: "This Constitution and the Laws of the United States which shall be made in Pursuance thereof; and all Treaties made, or which shall be made, under the Authority of the United States, shall be the supreme Law of the Land; and the Judges in every state shall be bound thereby, any Thing in the Constitution of Laws of any state to the contrary notwithstanding."[4] In other words, the Constitution established a limited federal system with the power to perform certain specified tasks. The federal government has the authority to regulate commerce, provide a uniform currency, provide uniform laws on bankruptcy, raise and support an Army and Navy, declare war, collect taxes, provide for the common defense, collect custom duties, and other powers vital to national well-being (see Article I, Section 8 for a complete listing of the federal government's powers), but leaves the majority of powers in the hands of the state governments and then to the people.

- *Limited Government.* The Founders made sure they carefully defined what the government could and could not do. They envisioned limited government and developed a document—the Constitution—to ensure government would be limited. The limitations on the federal government are contained in Article I, Section 8 of the Constitution, Article I, Section 9, and the Bill of Rights. Article I, Section 8 lists what the federal government may do. Article I, Section 9 lists what the federal government may not do. The Bill of Rights—the first ten amendments to the Constitution—provide important protections for the individual from the national government, and protects the powers retained by the states.

- *Barriers to Pure Majority Rule.* Concerned about the potential abuses of pure majority rule—mob rule—the Founders included several safeguards in the Constitution to preclude majoritarian democracy. These safeguards include a bicameral legislative branch (a Congress consisting of a Senate and a House of Representatives), unelected judiciary, limits on the powers of the federal government, indirect election of the president (electoral college), and various checks and balances, including federalism—a system of separation of power with checks and balances between the state and federal governments. Because of this we chafe at the seemingly ubiquitous references to the United States of America as a democracy. We are a constitutional republic. The Democrats would love for our Constitution to be replaced with a pure democracy they can control, the ultimate mob rule.

- *Separation of Powers.* The Founders were concerned about misrule and excesses on the part of all three branches of government: executive, legislative, and judicial. They dealt with this problem by applying the concept of balanced government envisioned by the French philosopher Montesquieu. Balanced government is based on an awareness of the sinful nature of man and the danger in giving any one branch of government too much power. This danger is overcome by dividing the various powers of government and distributing them among the executive, legislative, and judicial branches of government. This separation of powers was codified in the Constitution with Article

I listing the legislative powers, Article II the executive powers, and Article III the judicial powers. The Founders also included many ways the three branches of government check each other by ensuring no branch of government can perform its duties solely on its own. Rather, each branch requires the cooperation of the other branches. For example, the Supreme Court can declare executive acts to be unconstitutional, but the president nominates judges to the Supreme Court. Congress enacts laws, but the president can veto them. The Supreme Court can declare acts of Congress unconstitutional, but federal judges must be confirmed by the Senate, Congress controls the Supreme Court's budget, and Congress can impeach federal judges. As Federalist 51 and others make clear, federalism provides a double security for the rights of the people by establishing a separation of powers as well as checks and balances between the national and state governments.

We hope this brief overview of constitutional principles provides a perspective concerning what is at stake in the battle over the sovereignty and integrity of the Constitution as presented in the remainder of this chapter. These fundamental constitutional principles are under attack from the Left.

SOVEREIGNTY OF THE CONSTITUTION

The Constitution was established as the supreme law of the land for the United States. No other law, treaty, or action may take precedence over the Constitution. Unfortunately, advocates of the so-called living Constitution—including Supreme Court justices—are moving ever closer to allowing international treaties and international law to supersede the Constitution.

For a treaty to be valid, it must conform to the Constitution because the Constitution is a higher legal authority than a treaty. The Constitution is what gives our government the legal authority to enter treaties, a fact that protects America's sovereignty when interacting with foreign powers. The sovereignty of the Constitution protects the sovereignty of the American people which is our authority to govern ourselves independent of foreign intervention.

International law consists of laws developed and ratified by other countries and organizations, which means American citizens have no voice in their development or ratification. Consent of the governed is a fundamental principle of the Constitution. Therefore, laws developed and enacted without the consent of the American people should not be applied to the American people. Unfortunately, because of the misdeeds of Leftist judges and politicians, international law is finding its way into American courtrooms.

Sovereignty and International Treaties

International treaties are supposed to be subservient to the Constitution which is the source of authority for government officials who enter treaties. Increasingly, Leftist elected officials are showing a propensity for putting international treaties over and above the Constitution. The best example of constitutional sovereignty versus international treaties is the Paris Climate Agreement.

The Paris Climate Agreement is a poorly designed international treaty aimed at controlling climate change. President Barack Obama signed the agreement without the consent of Congress on September 3, 2016, making the United States a party to the Agreement. The stated purpose of the Paris Climate Agreement is to reduce global greenhouse gas emissions with the broader goal of limiting global temperature increases. Honoring a campaign promise, Donald Trump took the United States out of the agreement when he took office in 2017.

When Joe Biden was elected, he by-passed Congress and the American people using an executive order to make the United States a party once again to the Paris Climate Agreement. On the surface, the goal of the agreement sounds beneficial, but when one delves into it, the reasons President Trump removed the United States from the agreement become obvious. The Heritage Foundation examined the Paris Climate Agreement in detail and found several reasons why the United States should not be a party to it. These reasons are as follows:[5]

- *The Paris Agreement is costly and ineffective.* The agreement is harmful to American citizens who have no say in our country being part of it. It will destroy hundreds of thousands of American jobs, destroy what is left of our manufacturing base, and eliminate $2.5 trillion in gross domestic product by 2035. Further, if every participating country meets its commitments for reducing greenhouse gas emissions, the global benefits will be zero. Add to this some countries—China in particular—have an unfortunate tendency to underreport their carbon dioxide emissions, thereby invalidating the agreement and its goals.
- *Paris Agreement wastes taxpayer dollars.* The agreement calls for the establishment of a Green Climate Fund that would collect $100 billion per year from participating countries. President Barack Obama by-passed Congress and the American people and sent—without authorization—$1 billion to the fund. The money went to demonstrably corrupt governments as opposed to governments in real need.
- *Paris Agreement is bad for American energy competitiveness.* The ability of American energy companies—conventional and renewable—to compete on the global stage depends on innovation. Nothing hinders innovation more than being strapped by the artificial rules and regulations of international treaties the American people had no voice in developing.

Sovereignty and International Law

One of the more disturbing trends in American jurisprudence is the new propensity of judges to introduce international law into their decisions. The rights of American citizens should never be determined by foreign courts or international law. Allowing international law to creep into American jurisprudence is a violation of Article III of the Constitution which clearly states judicial power: ". . . shall be vested in one Supreme Court, and in such inferior Courts as the Congress may from time to time ordain and establish."[6]

Increasingly, the issue of applying international law to American citizens is coming into play. The most illustrative example occurred not long ago when Spanish judges expressed their desire to arrest American politicians for war crimes if they dared visit Europe. As idiotic as this notion sounds, it is the logical extension of the concept of applying international law to American citizens.

Law professor Jeremy Rabkin explains the role Leftist American judges and politicians have played in creating an atmosphere in which such ludicrous ideas would even be suggested by Spanish judges: "This is preposterous. It is akin to piracy. And not only has our government not protested this nonsense, but it has contributed to building up an international atmosphere in which this sort of thing seems plausible—an atmosphere where the old idea of a jury of one's peers and the idea of Americans having rights under the Constitution give way to the notion of some hazy international standard of conduct that everyone in the world can somehow agree upon and then enforce on strangers."[7]

The notion of an international standard of conduct in a world that rejects God, which has so many different religions—all with different ethical teachings and practices, and which also accommodates anti-God religions such as secular humanism is foolhardy. It is also antithetical to individual rights, justice, and American liberty.

INTEGRITY OF THE CONSTITUTION

The integrity of the Constitution is a function of how it is interpreted by those empowered to do so. The battle over constitutional interpretation is between advocates of either originalism or the living Constitution. Only if the originalists win this battle will the integrity of the Constitution be restored. The integrity of the Constitution was on the mind of James Madison—the "father" of the Constitution—when he wrote a letter to Henry Lee:

> I entirely concur in the propriety of resorting to the sense in which the Constitution was accepted and ratified by the nation. In that sense alone it is the legitimate Constitution. . . . If the meaning of the text be sought in the changeable meaning of the words composing it, it is evident that the

shapes and attributes of the Government must partake of the changes to which the words and phrases of all living languages are constantly subject.[8]

Originalism tethers the decisions of judges to the original intent of our Founders and the original meaning of the words in the Constitution. The living-Constitution approach, on the other hand, opens the judiciary to arbitrary, reckless, and self-interested decisions. American society is like a floating balloon. As the winds change, the balloon moves in that direction. As the winds change again, the balloon also changes direction. If it is tethered tightly to a solid stake in the ground, the balloon can endure these constant changes in the wind without being blown away, but if it is not tethered it will be lost. The Constitution in its original intent and meaning is what tethers American society to the ground of reason.

Living-Constitution advocates like to claim the law of the land must change to match the on-going changes in American society, but they miss a crucial point here. Think of the Constitution as your home. Americans are constantly changing their homes—colors schemes, carpet, flooring, window treatments, and furniture—to accord with changes in fashion, taste, and financial status. The reason these changes can be made without undermining the integrity of the home is the solid foundation under it. If the foundation under your home is solid, you can make all the stylistic changes you want. But undermine the home's foundation and the changes will one day come crashing down around you. Advocates of the living Constitution are undermining the foundation of America's sovereignty, justice, and liberty.

In his landmark book *Liberty and Tyranny*, Mark Levin explains what is really behind the living Constitution point of view:

> The Statist considers the judiciary his clearest path to amassing authority, for through it he can proclaim what the law is without effective challenge or concern with the fleeting outcome of an election cycle. Moreover, the federal judiciary is populated with about one thousand lawyers—and the

Supreme Court a mere nine—making statist infiltration
easy. Even when holding high office in the executive or
legislative branches, the Statist today looks for ways to
enhance judicial authority at the expense of his own branch,
for in doing so he seeks to immunize his agenda from a
change in public attitudes. And the statist on the court toler-
ates representative government only to the extent that its
decisions reinforce his ends. Otherwise, he overrules it.[9]

PRESERVING THE CONSTITUTION AND BILL OR RIGHTS: WHAT YOU CAN DO

Even Americans who are not well-versed in the intricacies of the
Constitution are put off by the specter of international treaties and
international law being imposed on them. Americans have always
had an inherent suspicion of "entangling alliances" with foreign
countries. For many Americans, getting involved in the business of
foreign countries is bad enough, but letting them get involved in
our business is downright unacceptable.

This inherent mistrust of letting other countries influence what
happens in America works in favor of patriotic Americans who want
to save our country from the wiles of Leftist ideologues who want
to destroy it. Here are some things you can do to help preserve the
Constitution and Bill of Rights:

Read the Constitution and Learn What It Says

All too often, Leftist ideologues who are trying to undermine the
Constitution know the document better than patriotic Americans
who want to preserve it. This sad situation cannot be allowed to
persist. Equip yourself to fight back against those who want to
destroy America by reading the Constitution through over and over
until you know it well. Make note of where the federal government
has already grown beyond the limits established by the Constitution.
Whenever there is discussion of "limited government," it is the
Constitution that prescribes those limits. Join the discussion and
show others how the federal government already exceeds its constitutional limits.

Teach Your Children and Grandchildren the Constitution

Do not depend on schools to instruct your children and grandchildren the Constitution. Do it yourself. With Leftist ideologues in control of most America's public schools, your children might complete elementary and high school without the Constitution ever being mentioned. Worse yet, if the Constitution is taught, it is likely to be a distorted version riddled with Leftist interpretations that are at best inaccurate. The more likely scenario is what your children and grandchildren will learn about the Constitution in school is almost certain to be false.

Know How to Refute the Left's False Claim the Constitution Is a "Godless Document"

Because God has no place in the America they envision, Leftist ideologues tend to ignore the Declaration of Independence. To their chagrin, the Declaration contains several undeniable references to God including "Nature's God," the "Creator," the "Supreme Judge of the World," and "Divine Providence."[10] Because of these references to God, Socialists focus solely on the Constitution as America's founding document, referring to it as a "Godless document."

There are several problems with this claim. First, you cannot fully understand the Constitution without first understanding the Declaration. The Declaration establishes the philosophical foundation for the United States, the rational for our country's existence. Therefore, it contains explicit references to God. The United States is a nation established by Christians based on biblical principles and Christian values. The Constitution, on the other hand, is not a philosophical document. Rather, it is an instruction manual for how to establish and govern a nation that rests on the philosophical foundation set forth in the Declaration. The two documents go together and are inseparable.

Second, the Constitution—though it does not contain as many explicit references to God as the Declaration—does contain one such a reference. Leftist ideologues who claim the Constitution is a Godless document conveniently overlook the explicit reference to God contained in Article VII: "the year of our Lord."[11] If the Constitution is indeed a Godless document as the Left claims, what Lord does this phrase from Article VII refer to?

Finally, the Constitution cannot be fully or properly understood without placing it in the context of its development. That context was summarized succinctly and well by Reverend Dr. Jedediah Morse in 1784 when he wrote: "To the kindly influence of Christianity, we owe that degree of freedom and political and social happiness which mankind enjoys. . . . Whenever the pillars of Christianity shall be overthrown, our present republican forms of government, and all the blessings which flow from them, must fall with them."[12]

Make the Sovereignty and Integrity of the Constitution an Issue in Elections

Candidates are appointed to the federal judiciary by the President and confirmed or rejected by the Senate. This makes your participation in presidential and senatorial races not plainly important but critical. Support presidential candidates who commit to nominating only originalists to the federal bench. Support Senatorial candidates who commit to confirming only originalists to the federal bench. An unshakable commitment to preserving the original intent of the Founders and the original meaning of their words as written in the Constitution is essential for federal judges at all levels.

CHAPTER 4

REJECTING HISTORICAL REVISIONISM AND REFUTING THE LIES OF THE SECULAR LEFT (SOCIALISTS)

The biggest obstacles the secular Left faces and the one they fear the most in trying to destroy the America of our Founders are the true and recorded history of our country and our nation's Christian heritage. The unaltered history of the United States clearly and undeniably refutes the lies, distortions, and obfuscations Socialists are trying to foist on school children, college students, our military, and the American public at large. It also clearly demonstrates America has a strong Christian heritage. Together, these two factors stand in the way of everything secular Leftists are trying to accomplish with their war on America and Christianity.

Secular humanism and Christianity are two diametrically opposed worldviews; they cannot peacefully coexist. America was founded by Christians and built on a solid foundation of Christian principles and values. Christianity is antithetical to everything the secular Left believes and is trying to do. Therefore, to destroy the America of our Founders, the Left must first destroy our history. Secularists must rewrite America's history to exclude even a hint of Christian influence, and that is exactly what they are trying to do.

Unfortunately, Americans are notorious for their ignorance of U.S. history. Our ignorance of history can be attributed to the propensity of Americans to look to the future not the past, and the fact that secular Leftist ideologues control the public schools and most colleges and universities. These two facts have made it easier for secularists to deny our country's Christian heritage.

It is, therefore, essential for Americans who believe in the vision of our Founders and who want to preserve that vision to learn our nation's true history and embrace it. The First Principles and the values informing the Founders' vision will save our country from the Left.

THE LEFT'S PLAN FOR REWRITING AMERICA'S HISTORY

Socialists have a three-part plan for rewriting America's history in their own image. Part one of the plan involves writing a new—albeit fictional—history of America and substituting it for the true history. Part two of the plan involves employing one of the favorite stratagems of Hitler's Nazi propaganda minister, Joseph Goebbels: tell big lies and repeat them over and over until they are accepted as truth. The third and final part of the plan is to alter the historical record by expunging material the Left does not want known from history books and the public square.

Later in this chapter, we explain all three parts of the secular Left's plan for rewriting America's history as well as what you can do to help reject historical revisionism and refute the lies of the Left. But before getting into the details of the secular Left's plan and how to defeat it, we provide an overview of secularization, explain why so many Americans are buying into this destructive concept, and summarize the tragic consequences of secularization. Americans who want to help save our country must understand those who are trying to rewrite, alter, and distort our history and why they are so determined to do so.

SECULARIZATION: A DESTRUCTIVE CONCEPT

If you are going to stand up to and speak out against the secularization of American society, you need a comprehensive understanding of the concept. Secularization is the process of systematically eliminating God from the culture. It is accomplished by removing the Bible, prayer, Christian symbols, and Christian influence from a nation's institutions, the public square, and all aspects of daily life.

It is ironic that secularists have gained so strong a foothold in America. Our country's Founders were guided in every instance by biblical principles in the deliberations, decisions, and actions leading them to establish our nation. However, in the America of today secularists reject any Christian influence in matters of government, public policy, education, and daily life.

The secularization of America began long ago, but it didn't gain a foothold until 1947 when the Supreme Court handed down one of the most biased decisions in its history: the "separation of church and state" ruling in *Everson v. Board of Education*.[1] This decision overturned 150 years of legal precedent and is an example of legislating from the bench, a practice that amounts to unconstitutional judicial usurpation.

Continuing the practice of judicial usurpation, in 1962 the Supreme Court outlawed sponsored prayer in public schools in *Engel v. Vitale*.[2] SCOTUS followed that decision with another outlawing Bible reading in public schools in the case of *Abington School District v. Schempp*, 1963.[3] Both decisions were victories for secular humanists. These unconstitutional decisions enabled by *Everson v. Board of Education* gave secular activists the ammunition they needed to begin a frontal assault on Christianity in America.

A key principle of the secular humanist philosophy is moral relativism. Whereas Christians view right, wrong, truth, and falsity as absolute concepts established by God and revealed in Holy Scripture, moral relativists reject God's Word as the source of truth and claim there are no moral absolutes. To a moral relativist, right, wrong, truth, and lie are matters of individual choice; people decide for themselves what is right, wrong, true, or false based on their own set of personal beliefs, values, and more to the point, *desires*.

The ultimate source of truth for a moral relativist is the individual rather than the God of Holy Scripture. In other words, to secularists—based on their principle of moral relativism—each individual human being is his or her own god. Whereas

Christianity is the worship of the sovereign God of Holy Scripture, secularism is a manufactured religion in which men and women worship themselves.

Putting aside for the moment that moral relativists reject God as the ultimate source of what is right and true, one could drive a truck through the holes in the logic or, better said, lack of logic underlying their philosophy. For starters, to state there are no moral absolutes is to state an absolute. Said another way, moral relativists state absolutely there are no absolutes. Worse yet, they fail to see the glaring contradiction in this. Further, moral relativists do not really believe what they claim to believe in the first place. Their philosophy is riddled with inconsistencies and contradictions.

For example, moral relativists will admit individuals cannot decide for themselves if murder is wrong. The same goes for stealing (though that sense is weakening in places like San Francisco). To get around these kinds of inconsistencies in their philosophy, moral relativists claim anything an individual decides to do is right unless it harms someone else. But this is grasping at straws. For example, moral relativists support abortion despite the fact the child who is aborted, its mother, and society in general are all harmed.

The aborted child is not just harmed, he or she is murdered. Mothers are often harmed when they suffer post-abortion regret, depression, and other emotional and even health problems. Finally, society is doubly harmed. First, aborting thousands of unborn babies devalues human life and contributes, as a result, to such tragedies as gun violence, mass shootings, road rage, and suicide. Second, abortion robs society of an unknown number of individuals who might have changed the world for the better had they lived, individuals who might have become entrepreneurs, inventors, scientists, astronauts, political leaders, educators, physicians, pastors, writers, engineers, poets, or presidents.

It is hubris of the worst kind to claim individuals can do anything they want provided their actions do not harm anyone else. Who decides what is harmful to others or to society? Just because an individual thinks his actions are not harmful does not mean they are not. In many cases, the harm may not be readily apparent; it may not manifest itself until years later. This is often the case, for example, with post-abortion regret and depression. Individuals are not equipped to be God and make the kinds of decisions only God should make. This fact alone invalidates secular humanism and moral relativism.

WHY SO MANY AMERICANS ARE BUYING INTO SECULARISM

People without strong biblical convictions are easy prey for secularists because secular humanism appeals to the sinful nature of man. Secular humanists reject God not because they do not believe in him, but because they do not want to live in accordance with his Word. They are like the man who claims smoking does not cause cancer simply because he does not want to give up cigarettes. Secular humanism is a hedonistic belief system based on satisfying the self-centered desires of its individual proponents. Secular humanists believe if they want to do something, they should be able to do it without the inconvenience of the moral constraints emanating from Christianity.

Although its proponents deny the fact, secular humanism is a religion, one allowing individuals to be their own gods. Their guiding principle of moral relativism introduces several inconsistencies into the religion of secular humanism. As a result, secular humanists struggle to answer inconvenient questions raised by the principle of moral relativism, questions such as this: What happens when one secularist believes something is right and another believes it is wrong? How do secularists resolve these kinds of differences between and among the little gods who make up their constituent group? The answer to this question is simple: they cannot.

The principles of secularism are the opposite of the biblical principles upon which our nation was founded. America's Founders knew the Bible and what it teaches. This knowledge led them to adopt specific principles and values that helped shape America and make it the most powerful, prosperous, and free nation on earth. Traditional values associated with the biblical principles that guided our Founders include freedom, individual rights, justice, peace, equality, personal responsibility, upward mobility, fair competition,

free enterprise, the rule of law, self-determination, private property,
and service above self through charity and volunteerism.

Individual human beings who view the world through the lens
of self-interest are not capable of conceiving such selfless values.
These kinds of values run counter to human nature because human
nature is fallen and, thus, guided by sin. Only a Holy God who is
incapable of sin could be the originator of the kinds of values America's Founders embraced. The Founders did not originate the values
that made America great; they adopted them from the Word of God.

A key point of contention between Christians and secularists is
the sovereignty of God. Christians believe the individual rights
spelled out in the Constitution and Bill of Rights come from the
God of Holy Scripture. Secularists believe these rights come from
government. They also deny the authority of God, substituting
instead the authority of government to enforce their specious morality. As a result of wanting to be their own god, secularists are like
lost hikers stumbling around in a forest without a compass, unsure
of where they are or where they are going.

TRAGIC CONSEQUENCES OF SECULARIZATION

When they boarded the *Mayflower*, the Pilgrims were not seeking
adventure, wealth, or fame. Rather, they risked everything sailing
to America seeking something of much greater value to them: religious freedom. To be able to worship God without interference
from kings and queens or their minions meant more than life itself
to these intrepid early settlers.

After a difficult voyage of sixty-six days, the Pilgrims got off to
a shaky start in the new land, but they persevered and, with God's
help, endured. What began at Plymouth Rock on November 11,
1620, would eventually become the United States of America on
July 4, 1776. Of course, a long and costly war had to be fought
before the dream of America could become a reality. The new
nation described in philosophical terms in the Declaration of Independence and practical terms in the Constitution would be richly
blessed by God. Fast-forward to the present. Much has changed
since 1776 when thirteen American colonies declared their

independence from Great Britain, and the changes have not been for the better.

Ignoring or worse yet, denying our country's Christian heritage, many Americans today reject God. In addition, anti-God activists and organizations have used the courts, public schools, colleges, universities, textbook publishers, the entertainment industry, politics, and the media to chip away at our religious liberty, attempting thereby to remove God from the lives of Americans. These attacks have degraded the culture in destructive ways for all Americans, including the secularists who blindly employ them. As a result, all Americans are suffering the tragic consequences of secularization, including secularists.

Consider just a few of the problems resulting from the secularization of American society. Abortion is common, widespread, and "legal" up to the moment of birth. Worse yet, advocates of this heinous practice have even tried to legalize post-birth abortions. Drug abuse and alcoholism have reached epidemic proportions. Pornography, including child pornography, is ubiquitous. Gun violence, mass shootings, human trafficking, child abuse, teen suicide, and corruption in government and business are now so common they have become a normal part of the culture. In late 2021, there was a cancel culture move to eliminate Thanksgiving.

Even worse than the societal problems resulting from secularization is the attitude of secularists toward the church. The religion clause of the First Amendment was intended to protect the church from government, but secularists conveniently ignore this fact choosing instead to claim government and, in turn, the American people must be protected from religion. Secularists claim this need to protect people from religion gives government the right to control the church.

This distortion of the intent of the First Amendment was used by public officials to advance their secular agenda during the COVID-19 pandemic of 2020 and 2021. Governments in some states used concerns for public safety—people meeting in groups—to force churches to close their doors. Even churches applying all the precautions recommended by the government's own healthcare agencies were forced to close their doors.

At the same time, secular state officials allowed people to congregate in bars, frequent liquor stores, and shop at major retail outlets as if people in groups in these settings were somehow immune to COVID-19. Even more ironic or hypocritical, state, and municipal governments in numerous large cities allowed thousands of people to congregate for the purpose of demonstrating and rioting. Applying the most convoluted logic imaginable, secular public officials declared religious services nonessential but bars, liquor stores, and riots essential.

Those who reject God are in the ascendency in America. Secularism is on the rise and Christianity is in decline. Where the church once influenced society and established cultural norms, society is now influencing the church. As a result, cultural norms are now controlled by secular ideologues in government, education, the entertainment industry, and social media. Where education, government, the public square, the culture, and society in general were once strongly influenced by Christianity, that influence is in decline as increasing numbers of Americans join the secular-humanist movement and get their guidance from television, movies, and the internet rather than Holy Scripture.

As Christians, we cannot justify sitting back and ignoring what is happening all around us, nor can we justify surrendering a nation blessed by God to secular ideologues who reject him. Remaining silent in the face of evil is the same as condoning evil. If Christians do not unite with one voice and stand up to the onslaught of secularism, our churches are going to become like the Alamo, tiny fortresses surrounded by an enemy bent on their destruction.

God makes clear in his Word what is expected of Christians when faced with challenges such as the growth of secularism. In James 4:17 we read: "So whoever knows the right thing to do and fails to do it, for him it is sin." As Christians, we know the right thing to do. We are to strap on the armor of God, become Christian soldiers, and do the demanding work of reclaiming America for Christ. Christians who remain silent when they should speak up and who sit idly by when they should act are committing the very sin the apostle James warned about in his epistle to Jewish Christians.

INVENTING HISTORY: A REVISIONIST STRATEGEM OF THE LEFT

If you do not like America's history, invent a new one. This is precisely what secular ideologues are doing, and it is an effective ploy because they control most of America's public schools, colleges, and universities. Since they control the curriculums, textbook selection, and teaching methods employed in the nation's K–12 and higher education systems, slipping fictional history into the classroom is easy. Two of the worst, most destructive examples of fictional history written by Leftist ideologues who hate America and are determined to tear it down are *Critical Race Theory (CRT)* and the *1619 Project*.

Critical Race Theory (CRT)

Critical Race Theory (CRT) was developed as a counterpoint to the aims and goals of the civil rights movement in America. Civil rights pioneers and martyrs such as Dr. Martin Luther King Jr. sought equality for people of all races; CRT rejects the concept of equality as a pipedream that can never be realized because America is an inherently racist nation controlled by oppressive white supremacists.

Advocates of CRT want to substitute what they call equity for equality. Equity as used by CRT proponents is an example of semantic subterfuge, a favorite tactic of the Left. Semantic subterfuge means adopting an appealing name for an unappealing concept. It is what the Left does when they refer to abortion as a mere "procedure" or as an issue of "choice." Equity, as envisioned by CRT advocates, means government-coerced equal results as opposed to equal opportunity. Equity eliminates consideration of competition, talent, motivation, effort, and performance in favor of race, gender, and sexual orientation.

According to Zachary Faria, "Another *New York Times* piece . . . noted that critical race theory is riddled with historical inaccuracies and crafted on the false premise that the American Revolution was fought to preserve slavery."[4] This basic false premise, in turn, leads to several conclusions that are not simply wrong but destructive:

- Individuals are to be classified as either oppressors or oppressed based solely on race with whites labeled oppressors and people of color oppressed.
- Questioning any of CRT's premises makes one a racist and, in turn, the enemy.
- People of color have no chance to improve their lives in America because of "systemic racism" and "white privilege."
- Whether an individual's ideas are worthy of discussion depends on their adherence to the principles of CRT.
- One's place in society is predetermined by skin color.
- To question any aspect of CRT is tantamount to denying the existence of racism.

As a concept, CRT is riddled with philosophical and factual holes. To begin with, in a society as diverse as ours in America, nothing is more important to positive race relations than honest, open, and frank dialogue in which all parties may state their opinions without fear of being attacked or canceled. CRT promotes tribalism, encourages an us-against-them attitude based on race, and shuts down dialogue between and among the races. In doing these things, CRT is bad for people of all races and bad for America. It douses the fire under the melting pot necessary for the perpetuation of E Pluribus Unum. Therefore, many of its opponents are people of color.

CRT shuts out people who acknowledge the existence of racism, are opposed to it, and work hard to overcome it but do not accept the premises of the concept. To CRT advocates, you either accept the reality of white privilege and white oppression or you are an enemy not to be heard. To CRT advocates, Dr. Martin Luther King Jr., and other heroes of the civil rights movement were naïve fools, and the white pastors, lawyers, and individuals who supported the movement were condescending dupes.

The 1619 Project

The 1619 Project was developed by Nicole Hannah-Jones and the *New York Times* and published in August 2019. The project posits the sole reason for the founding of America was the perpetuation of slavery as an institution. Proponents of the 1619 Project claim America was founded not on the philosophical ideals of liberty and freedom set forth in the Declaration of Independence but out of racism and a desire to perpetuate the commercial buying and selling of human beings. Other claims of proponents of the 1619 Project include the following:

- American prosperity is based solely on the forced labor of slaves.
- Capitalism is an inherently exploitive system designed to impoverish people of color while enriching white people.
- Racism is the core value of American nationhood.

Not surprisingly, the 1619 Project has been widely criticized by historians and scholars of all races who have stated the project's narrative leaves out huge swaths of American history and distorts those parts of the historical record it does cover. Timothy Sandefur, writing for the Cato Institute, makes the excellent point that in claiming America's prosperity is based solely on the forced labor of black slaves its authors ignore the major contributions made by immigrants from China, Japan, Ireland, and Europe.[5] It also ignores the contributions of white Americans who never owned slaves. According to Sandefur, "What was unique about America was that its founding marked the very first time that a nation was expressly founded on principles incompatible with slavery. Little wonder that the world's first anti-slavery society was established in Philadelphia in 1775."[6]

During a White House history conference in September 2020, President Donald Trump summarized the problems with the 1619 Project in these words: "The Left has warped, distorted, and defiled the American story with deceptions, falsehoods, and lies. There is no better example than the *New York Times* discredited 1619 Project. This project rewrites American history to teach our children that we were founded on the principle of oppression, not freedom."[7] To counter the 1619 Project, President Trump established the 1776 Commission, but the Commission was disbanded by President Joe Biden on his first day in office.

THE LEFTS'S "BIG LIE" STRATEGY

In making war on God and America, secular Socialists have adopted some of the same despicable tactics used by Adolph Hitler and his Nazi minions in World War II. One of these tactics is known as the "big lie." Often attributed to Hitler's propaganda minister, Joseph Goebbels, the big lie is explained as follows: "If you tell a lie big enough and keep repeating it, people will eventually come to believe it. The lie can be maintained only for such time as the State can shield the people from the political, economic and/or military consequences of the lie. It thus becomes vitally important for the State to use all of its powers to repress dissent, for the truth is the mortal enemy of the lie . . ."[8]

A psychological profile of Hitler done by the Organization of Strategic Services (OSS) during World War II described how he used the big lie. The profile should be familiar to anyone who has to deal with the Leftist ideologues who are trying to destroy America: "His primary rules were: never allow the public to cool off; never admit a fault or wrong; never concede that there may be some good in your enemy; never accept blame; concentrate on one enemy at a time and blame him for everything that goes wrong; people will believe a big lie sooner than a little one; and if you repeat it frequently enough people will sooner or later believe it."[9]

In adopting this deceptive tactic, the Left substitutes its movement for the state. Everything else about the tactic remains the same, particularly repressing dissent. The secular Left has carefully selected several big lies that, if accepted as truth by the American public, undermine opposition to their cause of destroying what our Founders established. Americans who want to play a positive role in saving our country from the Left should know these lies and be able to refute them with the truth because, as Goebbels rightly observed, ". . . the truth is the mortal enemy of the lie."[10]

Big Lie Number 1: Jesus Was a Socialist

Of all the numerous examples of how secular Leftists distort facts to support their anti-Christian, anti-American agenda while ignoring facts that run counter to Leftist orthodoxy, the lie that stands out above all the rest is Jesus was a socialist. Socialists like to use the Bible against Christians. Because Jesus is the foundation of Christianity, if the Left can undermine his credibility, they can destroy Christianity and render America's Christian heritage moot.

In claiming Jesus was a socialist, Leftist ideologues base their absurd claim on his concern for the poor throughout the New Testament. They like to quote Matthew 19:21 to "prove" Jesus was a socialist. In Matthew 19, a rich young man approaches Jesus to inquire what he must do to have everlasting life. Jesus tells the man he must follow the Commandments. The man claims he has always done so. Knowing the man's heart, Jesus then tells him: "If you would be perfect, go, sell what you possess and give to the poor, and you will have treasure in heaven; and come follow me."

Secular Leftists purposefully twist the meaning of Matthew 19:21 to show Jesus was an advocate of the redistribution of wealth, which is semantic subterfuge for the government taking everyone's money and doling it out as government officials see fit—a cornerstone principle of socialism. But this is hardly the message Matthew 19:21 conveys. Rather, Jesus told the man to give all he had to the poor to expose the man's insincerity and selfishness.

He knew the man was not willing to give up his wealth. Telling him to do so was not an endorsement of government redistribution of wealth. He told him to give away his wealth voluntarily. The man had many neighbors who were poor and could have used his help. By telling the man to help the poor, Jesus exposed the man's selfish heart.

Voluntarily giving to the poor is a fundamental principle of Christianity, not socialism. Redistribution of wealth, a fundamental tenet of socialism, amounts to government confiscation and redistribution of wealth by coercion. It is not a voluntary concept. The government takes your money through taxation whether you want to give it or not and redistributes it as government bureaucrats deem appropriate, often into their own pockets.

It is easy to see why the Left conjured up this lie and repeats it so often. What better way to give credibility to one's views than to claim Jesus shared them? This, of course, is what Socialists are trying to do by claiming Jesus was a socialist. There is a lot of irony in Socialists using Jesus to validate their nefarious views since they reject him and everything he stands for. The Bible cautions against this presumptuous practice in Romans 1:22–23: "Claiming to be wise, they became fools, and exchanged the glory of the immortal God for images resembling mortal man . . ." Secular Leftists who claim Jesus was a socialist are the kinds of fools referred to in Romans 1:22–23.

Big Lie Number 2: Opponents of the Left Are Racists

There is a joke that the shortest time known to man is the time between when the light turns green and the driver behind you beeps his horn. As short as this span of time usually is, there is one even shorter. It happens when debating a Leftist. It is the amount of elapsed time in the debate before the Leftist ideologue calls you a racist. Claiming opponents of Leftist orthodoxy are racists is a favorite ploy of losers who cannot support their ideas and opinions using logic, reason, facts, or common sense.

Those who fought to establish civil rights in America must roll over in their graves because of how the term *racist* is used today. The misuse of this term has robbed it of its meaning and value. During the civil rights movement of the 1960s, in certain parts of the South, real racists set snarling police dogs on peaceful demonstrators, blew up a church killing little black girls, ran down marchers and beat them with clubs, poured food over the heads of people conducting sit-ins at segregated restaurants, and turned firehoses on protestors.

These acts of violence were blatantly racist. Now all it takes to be labeled a racist is to disagree with a Leftist on any issue. The term *racist* is no longer used to describe people who discriminate based on race and who abuse people of color. It is used to gain political advantage and to scare away dissenters who do not want to be labeled racists. As a result, a term that is supposed to describe a vile, contemptible person is being fully devalued. Ironically, you now have white Leftists who have never experienced racial discrimination calling successful black Americans who have experienced it racists simply because they do not buy what the Left is trying to sell.

Socialists who hypocritically and deceitfully misuse the term *racist* to gain political advantage or bludgeon opponents rather than engaging in open, honest, frank dialogue only widen the racial divide and perpetuate racism. This is precisely what the Left wants to happen. It is part of their divide-and-conquer strategy. If the Left can convince racial groups they are perpetual victims and portray themselves as advocates for these oppressed minorities, they can perpetuate racial discord and use it to their advantage in making war on God and America.

To counteract the underhanded machinations of the Left, Americans who want to help save our country can do several things. First, do not allow yourself to be labeled a racist just because you disagree with a Leftist. When called a racist by a Leftist ideologue, calmly explain your views on race come from the example of Christ. People of all races are Christ's children, and he loves them all. This being the case, so do you.

When debating Leftists who try to play the race card, explain how the way to eliminate racism is not to point fingers or call people names. Rather, it is to look for common ground between people of different races. Tell Socialists the most effective form of common ground is a shared belief in God. People of different races who put God at the center of their lives have common ground that transcends racial differences. Further, viewing people of different races as individuals will help bring racial reconciliation while viewing them as members of racial groups—as Socialists do—just ensures racial discord.

Big Lie Number 3: Opponents of the Left Are Intolerant

Leftists turn the concept of tolerance on its head. When they claim Christians and Conservatives are intolerant, secular Socialists are engaging in what psychologists call *transference*. Transference means attributing to others that of which you are guilty. Tolerance is a willingness to hear opinions different from your own—opinions you might disagree with—and to acknowledge the right of other people to hold those opinions. Tolerant people can disagree without being disagreeable. Being tolerant is a sign of intelligence and maturity.

Not surprisingly, the least tolerant people on the planet are Leftist ideologues. To them, tolerance means coerced conformance to Leftist orthodoxy. Here are a few examples of Leftist "tolerance." Conservative and Christian speakers are shouted down, harassed, and even attacked on college campuses by Leftist students who do not want to hear what they have to say and do not want anyone else to hear it either.

Social media users who make statements at odds with Leftist orthodoxy are attacked, vilified, and even canceled by having their accounts shut down. Newspaper reporters are fired for writing articles the Left deems politically incorrect. Businesses are boycotted for failing to jump on the Leftist bandwagon. Military personnel are disciplined and even drummed out of the service for questioning the LBGTQ worldview being pushed on them from above. The Left's distorted interpretation of tolerance is the most serious challenge to free speech and free thought in America's history. Therefore, it is important for patriots who want to save our country to push back against the intolerance of the Left.

When confronted by the distorted version of Leftist "tolerance," be prepared to explain what tolerance really means and ask the person confronting you what he or she is afraid of. Make the point that real tolerance is a sign of intelligence and maturity. If people are supremely comfortable with their views, they are not afraid to hear other views and they can interact with people who hold different views without being disagreeable.

When you are attacked on social media by Leftist ideologues, simply ignore their venomous statements. You do not need their approval, and something would be amiss if you received their approval. If a social media platform cancels your account, contact your congressional representative and senators right away. Elected officials on both sides of the aisle in Congress are unhappy with the big-tech companies controlling and manipulating access to social media. Add your voice to the chorus of unhappy citizens who believe these big-tech firms should be regulated or broken up or both.

Big Lie Number 4: Stricter Gun Control Laws Will Eliminate Gun Violence

Listen to the rhetoric of the Left and you would think guns are the world's greatest evil. Leftist orthodoxy claims all America must do to end gun violence is take all guns away from Americans—not just criminals, but all Americans. To Leftist ideologues, the Founders got it wrong when they included the Second Amendment in the Constitution.

For the past sixty years, the Second Amendment has repelled the ongoing attacks from the Left. The U.S. Supreme Court has consistently upheld the right of Americans to own firearms and use them for such applications as hunting, target practice, and defending life and property. Further, the Supreme Court has ruled that local and state governments are held to the same restrictions as the federal government in limiting gun ownership and use.

The Supreme Court notwithstanding, Leftist ideologues will continue to challenge the Second Amendment and attack gun ownership by private citizens. Consequently, Americans who want to preserve and protect the Constitution and the right of gun ownership must be prepared to respond in an informed and logical manner to attacks on the Second Amendment. The following facts may be used to refute the gun-control agenda pushed by the Left:

- Since criminals do not obey laws—that is why we call them criminals—if the government confiscates guns, only criminals will have guns. Gun-control laws harm only innocent, law-abiding citizens while failing to deter criminals or decrease gun violence. If guns are outlawed in the United States, criminals will simply smuggle them in through our wide-open southern border.
- If law-abiding Americans are not allowed to own guns, they will have no way of protecting themselves and their families from criminals who do have guns. With home invasions at an all-time high, the probability of needing a gun for protecting one's family is high.
- Chicago has stricter gun-control laws than most cities, yet it remains the murder capital of America with the rate of gun-violence incidents increasing every year.

- Guns do not kill people; they are just inanimate objects. Criminals kill people using not just guns but knives, baseball bats, bricks, crowbars, screwdrivers, their bare hands, and other weapons of opportunity. Should the Supreme Court be asked to ban everything that can be used to kill?

Big Lie Number 5: America's Christian Heritage Is a Myth

No serious student of American history would deny our nation's Christian heritage. The evidence is too conclusive, persuasive, and ubiquitous. Even a cursory review of the unaltered historical record reveals mountains of corroborating evidence. This evidence can be found in inscriptions carved in stone in our nation's capital as well as the words of our Founding Fathers, early presidents, and early Supreme Court justices. The brief overview of America's Christian heritage presented herein only scratches the surface of what is available to anyone interested in knowing the truth rather than denying or distorting it.

A visit to our nation's capital, Washington, DC, will reveal enough Christian references carved in stone to fill a book. Inside the Washington Monument you will find such phrases as "Holiness to the Lord," "Search the Scriptures," and "In God We Trust," carved into the walls. In the Capitol, the phrase "In God We Trust" is carved into the wall above the Speaker's rostrum in the House of Representatives. At the east entrance of the Senate Chamber, you will find the words "Annuit Coeptis," which is Latin for "God has favored our undertakings." At the southern entrance to the Senate Chamber, the words "In God We Trust" are inscribed on the wall.

The historical record is replete with Christian statements made or written by our Founding Fathers. One of the best examples comes from Benjamin Franklin because secular Leftists like to claim Franklin as an unbeliever. His words suggest otherwise. Benjamin Franklin may have saved our fledgling nation from failing before it even got started by reminding his fellow delegates to the Constitutional Convention of the words contained in Psalm 127:1. It was May 1787. General Washington and his citizen soldiers finally defeated the British. The next challenge faced by the Founders was developing the Constitution, but things were not going well. There was much disagreement among the delegates and tempers were flaring.

It was at this point an aged and ailing Franklin took the floor and made the following statement:

> I have lived, sir, a long time, and the longer I live, the more convincing proofs I see of this truth: that God governs in the affairs of men. And if a sparrow cannot fall to the ground without His notice, is it probable that an empire can rise without His aid? We have been assured, sir, in the sacred writings that 'except the Lord builds the house, they labor in vain who build it.' I passionately believe this; and I also believe without His concurring aid we shall succeed in this political building no better than the builders of Babel.[11]

The words of our first two presidents debunk the claim of secular Leftists that America's Christian heritage is a myth. In his Thanksgiving Proclamation on October 3, 1789, George Washington, America's first president, said: "It is the duty of all nations to acknowledge the providence of Almighty God, to obey His will, to be grateful for His benefits, and humbly to implore His protection and favor."[12] Speaking to the Massachusetts militia on October 11, 1798, Washington's successor, John Adams, made the following statement: "Our Constitution was made only for a moral and religious people. It is wholly inadequate to the government of any other."[13]

The first Chief Justice of the U.S. Supreme Court was John Jay. Jay made his views on America's Christian heritage known on October 12, 1816, he said: "Providence has given to our people the choice of their rulers, and it is the duty, as well as the privilege and interest of our Christian nation, to select and prefer Christians for their rulers." Like Washington and Adams, Jay was clearly a Christian who viewed the United Sates as a nation based on Christian principles.

Big Lie Number 6: People Have the Right to Choose Their Own Sex

What better way to undermine God's influence on society than to encourage people to violate the natural order God has established for society? Socialists are exploiting the transgender movement in America for this very purpose. The Left's message when it comes to an individual's sex is this: You can choose your own sex by merely identifying with the sex you would like to be. This is hubris of the worst kind, another demonstration that secular Leftists believe individuals are their own gods. They even apply this absurd claim to young children not yet mature enough to cross the street by themselves. Not surprisingly, Socialists also claim parents have no say in the matter.

One of the saddest aspects of the transgender concept is the number of corporations who meekly join the cause to support this big lie. Large corporations coming out in favor of people simply choosing the sex they identify with are worse than hypocrites. Their board members do not truly support the concept; they are just afraid to admit it. What they support are profits. These corporate cowards are afraid the negative publicity Leftist ideologues might generate and the boycotts they might undertake will undermine profits.

To a secular Leftist, a man who identifies as a woman is, in fact, a woman and a woman who identifies as a man is, in fact, a man. This is the basis for the major controversy enveloping women's sports. Transgender men who have an undeniable physical advantage over women are insisting on competing against biological women. Not surprisingly, they are winning most of the athletic events.

Women who have worked hard all their lives to make the Olympic team or win a college scholarship are being robbed of their opportunities by men who identify as women. Sadly, most major sports associations and women's rights groups have caved to the pressure from the Left and are allowing this travesty to go forward. Biological women are beginning to speak up and fight back, but the deck is stacked against them in today's WOKE culture.

Americans who want to save our country from the Left must confront this big lie with God's truth. Here is a summary of that truth. An individual's sex is determined by biological processes put in place by God, not by personal preference. Men have one X and one Y chromosome while women have two X chromosomes. No amount of lipstick or surgery will change a man's XY chromosomes to XX chromosomes and vice-versa. Further, unless a man can somehow manage to undergo childbirth or endure monthly menstrual pains, he has no right to claim to be a woman. Man is not empowered to change what God has ordained. If Socialists think a man can be a woman, let them try to get milk from a bull or an egg from a rooster.

A question you might ask Leftist transgender advocates is this: If people can choose their own sex, why can't they choose their own race? Leftist ideologues run from this question like a house on fire because they are afraid of angering the black community. Black Americans have rightly resisted allowing people of other races to identify as black because people who want to do this have not walked in the shoes of a black person nor can they.

ALTERING THE HISTORICAL RECORD

Working together with the secular Leftist professors who write the history books, Leftist ideologues are altering the historical record by expunging material they object to. Anything about America that does not accord with Leftist orthodoxy is simply erased. It is not included in the history textbooks used by children in the public K–12 system or in higher education. One could fill many books with those parts of the historical record omitted from contemporary history textbooks. A classic example of this despicable practice is the story of the Pilgrims and their voyage on the *Mayflower*.

Tired of suffering persecution for refusing to accept the religion mandated by European monarchs, the Pilgrims banded together and risked everything to start new lives on a new continent. They sailed on a tiny ship—the *Mayflower*—across the Atlantic Ocean to North America, their intention being to land on the coast of Virginia. Every man and woman on board was determined to begin a new life and practice his or her own religion without interference, coercion, or persecution from kings, queens, or their minions.

After a rough voyage in which they were blown well off course, the Pilgrims anchored offshore from Plymouth, far north of their intended destination. Nevertheless, these intrepid Pilgrims decided they would start their new lives where God planted them. The place they landed became Plymouth Colony, then Massachusetts Bay Colony, and eventually the state of Massachusetts. Their first order of business was developing a governing document called the Mayflower Compact. The most important paragraph in that document is expunged from modern history textbooks if the Mayflower Compact is mentioned at all. It reads as follows:

> Having undertaken for the glory of God, and advancement of the Christian faith, and honor of our king and country, a voyage to plant the first colony in the northern parts of Virginia, do by these presents solemnly and mutually, in the presence of God, and one another, covenant and combine our selves together into a civil body politic . . .[14]

One can easily see why secular authors and publishers either censor this portion of the Mayflower Compact or omit the entire document from history books. The Mayflower Compact leaves no doubt concerning the views of early European settlers on Christianity. Their plan was to advance the Christian faith and plant a colony in northern Virginia governed according to biblical principles.

Although they were well off course in reaching their planned destination, they were right on course when it came to building a colony on a foundation of Christianity. The Pilgrims sought neither fame nor fortune. Rather, they sought to honor God and secure religious freedom for themselves and their families. The Mayflower Compact is just one example of many in which the truth requires secularists to alter the historical record.

REJECTING THE HISTORICAL REVISIONISM OF SECULARISTS

At this point you have sufficient information to understand why it is important to embrace the truth about America's history. But what should you do with this information? How can you use what you now know to reject historical revisionism and refute the big lies of the Left? The answer to this question, although simple to state, will not be easy to conduct. Americans who want to save America from destruction by the Left must unite and become as active in fighting against historical revisionism as proponents of this nefarious practice are in carrying it out.

Specifically, believers need to push back against historical revisionism in education from kindergarten through college. The motto of Americans who want to restore the vision of our Founders must be "Stand up and speak out." One of the reasons God has been removed from public education in America is too many Christians remained silent as it was happening. We have not been as determined in defending Christianity as secularists have been in attacking it.

If your children attend public schools, find out what they are being taught. Read their textbooks and determine if these books accurately and fully present the truth about America's history and the Founder's vision. If not, which is the case, stand up and speak out. Demand the school board put an end to Marxist indoctrination and dumbing down of the curriculum. Remind school officials your taxes pay their salaries. If school officials refuse your demands, take your children out of public schools, and enroll them in Christian schools or homeschool them. Nothing gets the attention of school boards like declining enrollments.

Taking on the public school establishment may sound like a daunting task, but it is already being done in local communities throughout the country. Never forget that as a taxpayer you pay for public education, even if your children do not attend public schools. An example of what individuals can do when they band together can be found in Johnson County, North Carolina. In response to pressure from concerned parents, the Johnson County school board adopted a policy that calls for disciplining or even firing teachers who incorporate Critical Race Theory (CRT) into the curriculum.[15]

If your children plan to attend college, help them choose wisely. Attending a certain college or university because they like the athletic program, it is where friends plan to attend, or it is Mom's or Dad's alma mater is not wise. Find out if your children will be required to attend indoctrination sessions on such topics as same-sex attraction and transgenderism in the name of "inclusion." Find out if the institution in question has designated "free-speech zones" that are really used to restrict free speech, particularly that of Christian and conservative students.

Find out if the institution in question punishes students for using terms it deems politically incorrect and if it labels biblical terms as hate speech. Examine the curriculum for the program of study your children will pursue and talk to professors who teach in that program. Find out up front if they are truly educators or Leftist ideologues masquerading as educators. Contact Alliance Defending Freedom (adflegal.org) and find out if the institution in question has been sued by Christian students for discriminatory or repressive practices against believers.

If it appears the college or university your children want to attend is controlled by secular Socialists pushing an anti-God agenda, step back and rethink your plans. It makes no sense to pay the enormous costs of college only to have Marxist professors spend four years or more turning your children into the next generation of Leftist ideologues who reject God. It might be necessary to attend a different college, a Christian college. College is too expensive and too influential an experience to take lightly. Why pay Marxist professors to indoctrinate your children in ideological nonsense while robbing them of the education they need to build better lives for themselves?

One more thing about colleges and universities. No matter how much you love your alma mater, if it has become a hot bed of secular activism and a center of Leftist indoctrination since you graduated, do not respond to the inevitable letters of request for donations. Why provide financial support to an institution doing everything in its power to undermine your beliefs, transform your children into secular minions, and drive God out of your daily lives? Why help an institution replace the Founder's Christian vision with the anti-God vision of secularists?

Refusing to support a secular institution financially is important, but it is not enough. In addition, send a letter to the president of the institution explaining why further financial support from you will not be forthcoming. Nothing gets the attention of a college or university president faster than money. Secularists get away with their unrelenting attacks on God and country as well as such underhanded practices as historical revisionism because these things cost them nothing. If they must pay a price for their twisted beliefs and nefarious practices, secularists will be forced to step out of the fantasyland they inhabit and face some hard realities. Making this happen is the duty of Americans who want to save our country from the Left.

CHAPTER 5

PRESERVING CAPITALISM– REJECTING SOCIALISM

A major strategy in the Left's war on God and country is convincing Americans to reject free-market capitalism in favor of socialism, a flawed and failed philosophy everywhere it has been tried. It failed in the Soviet Union and Cambodia. It is currently failing in Cuba, North Korea, and Venezuela. It was failing in China and Viet Nam until these two countries got partially smart and began allowing private enterprise, free markets, and entrepreneurship.

For decades, Leftist ideologues have used indoctrination, deception, and distortion to convince naïve Americans that socialism is superior to capitalism. They have focused on school children and college students to teach the manifestly false claim that government is the answer to all problems. Socialists seduce naïve young people with promises of free college tuition, free healthcare, and a free ride through life. Socialism is not presented as complete government control over every aspect of the individual's life—which it is—but as caring nanny government seeking only to take care of people.

The bigger lie told by the Left is government can take care of them from cradle to grave. Government could not do this in the Soviet Union or Cambodia, and it cannot do it now in Cuba, North Korea, or Venezuela where chronic shortages of essential goods and services, electrical blackouts, and abominably poor healthcare are the norm.

What happens under a socialist regime is predictable. To follow through on its promises of free everything, the government increases taxes over and over until the people have no more taxes to give. The more people are taxed, the less incentive they have to work, produce, and contribute so they become unproductive drains on the economy. The less productive people become, the fewer goods they produce and the fewer services they provide. This causes chronic scarcity which, in turn, drives prices up causing inflation. Inflation robs the currency of its value and soon a shopping cart full of cash will not buy a loaf of bread. This is precisely where things stand in socialist Venezuela now where people are fighting over scraps of food from trash cans while the bloated bureaucrats who run the government live in luxury. This is socialism!

PROBLEMS WITH SOCIALISM

History has shown socialism is a flawed concept that simply does not work. It encourages corruption and tyranny, is grounded in economic illiteracy, and robs people of their individual rights, freedoms, and liberty. As it relates to the subject of this book—saving America from the Left—the biggest problem with socialism is it eliminates individual incentives, thereby robbing people of initiative, drive, ambition, entrepreneurship, and the other personal assets that make them and, in turn, a nation productive. It replaces these assets with an entitlement mentality.[1]

It is this aspect of socialism—encouragement of an entitlement mentality—we focus on in this chapter. Our reason for this focus is because the Left knows the current generation of young people in America is the most entitled, work-averse generation in our nation's history. Young people today have been given so much—often by helicopter parents—they now feel entitled. What they have not been given is responsibility, accountability, or the need to work for anything. As a result, they have not developed a strong work ethic, the work ethic of Americans who have contributed so much to our country's productivity and quality of life. A lot of young Americans are spoiled, and feel entitled to anything they desire. This makes them especially susceptible to the promises of a free ride by socialist ideologues.

THE ENTITLEMENT MENTALITY AND SOCIALISM

Because of the way young people have been raised over the past sixty years coupled with the inclusive policies of Leftist public schools in which everybody wins, everybody makes the team, and everybody get a trophy, they have come to believe they should be handed what previous generations had to work hard for. As a result, the entrepreneurial spirit and traditional work ethic have been supplanted by an entitlement mentality—a mentality inculcated by the pushers of socialism.

The disease of entitlement is antithetical to everything that made America great. Worse yet, it is self-inflicted. It originated in homes where overindulgent parents—also known as helicopter parents—gave their children everything they could need except what they needed most: a belief in the traditional American values of thrift, diligence, self-reliance, self-discipline, responsibility, accountability, deferred gratification, and demanding work.

Children who were raised in this kind of environment grew up to become pampered adults who expect the federal government to replace their parents in providing for their every want and whim. This makes them especially susceptible to the false claims of Leftist ideologues trying to recruit them into socialism. When a nanny government reinforces the entitlement mentality by offering handouts, the entrepreneurial spirit and traditional work ethic are eroded further, and the disease of entitlement becomes more resistant to a cure.

SOCIALISM IS MORE THAN JUST A MISGUIDED ECONOMIC SYSTEM

An economist will define socialism as a centrally planned economy in which the government controls the means of production and distribution. This is a sterile definition not unlike defining inoperable cancer as just an illness. Socialism is much more than just an economic system. It is a worldview based on the premise the state knows best what you should think and how you should live. Socialism results in complete government control of all aspects of the economy as well as the individual's life. In the process, socialism reduces productive, contributing people to the same level as those who are less productive and contribute little or nothing to the economy.

With socialism, the state is supreme, and all problems have the same solution: government. In a socialist system, individual responsibility is replaced by group responsibility, meaning no one is responsible. When no one is responsible, things do not get done and a nation's productivity plummets. With socialism, Christian charity is replaced by government-enforced redistribution of wealth, which in practical terms means taking money in the form of taxation from productive people and giving it to unproductive people.

Government handouts are not charity; they are legalized theft. When the state becomes supreme and government becomes the solution, the enterprising spirit, work ethic, freedom, and liberty quickly become casualties. A lot of Americans—particularly college-aged individuals—are buying into socialism and killing the American spirit.

In 2021, Democrats controlled the White House and Congress, and socialist ideologues controlled the Democrats. This unfortunate combination led to a series of government handouts falsely labeled "stimulus checks" being sent to individual Americans under the misleading name the "American Rescue Plan." These stimulus checks did nothing to stimulate an economy struggling with the COVID-19 pandemic. In fact, they had the opposite effect. If recipients got their government checks in the mail, they refused to work creating the unprecedented situation in which hundreds of thousands of jobs went unfilled and businesses had to cut back on their hours of operation. Many businesses, unable to find employees, went out of business.

A rapidly growing federal government is pushing our country ever deeper into the murky swamp of socialism where restrictions on individual freedom are the norm, the entrepreneurial spirit is drowned in bureaucratic muck, and the traditional work ethic is replaced by an entitlement mentality. To save our country from the

Leftist ideologues who are bent on destroying it, we must reject socialism in favor of the values that formed and built this nation into the freest and most prosperous ever seen.

MOST CRITICAL STEP IN REJECTING SOCIALISM

The most critical step in rejecting socialism is accurately diagnosing the problem. It is important for Americans who want to save our country from the Left to understand the problem is first one of character and second one of economics. The late economist Walter Williams expressed this view in his syndicated column when he wrote: "Most of our nation's great problems, including our economic problems, have as their root decaying moral values."[2] Williams was prescient in that the factors that placed our country on the slippery slope to socialism relate more to character than to economics.

America has accumulated a massive national debt because an increasingly socialist government is doing things our Founders never intended it to do. The government is doing what all socialist governments do: spend more than they bring in and cover the difference by borrowing. The spend, spend, spend mentality so deeply rooted in Washington, DC came about because Americans lost their moral bearings.

The traditional American values of thrift, diligence, self-reliance, self-discipline, personal responsibility, accountability, deferred gratification, and hard work, when taken together, define character and are the foundation of the ambitious spirit and the traditional work ethic. The entrepreneurial spirit and traditional work ethic are, in turn, the best antidotes to the entitlement mentality. Consequently, a critical step in reversing America's downhill slide into socialism is to reestablish these values. Reestablishing these values is so important a part of saving America from the Left, they must be examined in greater detail here:

- *Thrift.* At one time, Americans would scrimp and save to buy the things they wanted but could not afford. In those bygone days, savings accounts were common, and layaway was standard practice. But with the advent of credit cards, Americans who wanted to *supersize* their lives adopted a buy-now-and-worry-about-it-later attitude. This attitude and the ease of buying on credit institutionalized the practice of living beyond one's means. As a result, Americans are drowning in a sea of debt they have little hope of paying off. This is one of the reasons few Americans question the government's continual spending creating a gargantuan national debt. Being over one's head in debt has become a way of life in America for individuals and the government.

- *Diligence.* Pride of workmanship used to be an indigenous American trait. A popular maxim in years past was *anything worth doing is worth doing right.* However, over the years, pride of workmanship has been replaced by a lax attitude leading to the coining of another less admirable maxim: *it is good enough for government work.* It is difficult for American companies to compete on the global stage when their employees have lax attitudes toward quality and take no pride in their workmanship.

- *Self-reliance.* In years past, self-reliance was as American as baseball. Our country was able to span the continent from the Atlantic to the Pacific only because early Americans were a self-reliant breed. *Do it yourself* was a popular phrase illustrating the typical American's attitude toward the everyday challenges of life. However, the teaching of socialistic doctrine in America's colleges, universities, and public schools, the overindulgence of helicopter parents, and the rapid expansion of the service sector combined to create a dependent generation that grew accustomed to having others do for them the things they should do for themselves. The logical extension of this attitude is to become dependent on the government rather than on individual initiative, which is precisely what the Left wants for American citizens.

- *Self-discipline.* Americans used to be a more disciplined society. We patiently saved for things we could not yet afford, made meals from scratch, and dressed up for church and other special occasions. Self-discipline has since been replaced by a hedonistic self-centeredness in which Americans demand immediate gratification for their every want and whim. Credit cards, fast food, and other innovations eliminate waiting, combined with an attitude of "it's-all-about-me," have undermined self-discipline in America. Why save up for something when you can have it right now with just the swipe of a credit card? Why not purchase more house than you can afford when the government will bail you out if you default on the payments? Why make healthy meals from scratch when you can get unhealthy meals in seconds at a drive-through window? Why call someone back later when you can simply answer your cell phone right now, even if you are in the middle of a movie or a meeting? Why should I worry about the problems my lack of self-discipline will create when the government just bails me out to pass those problems on to future generations? Finally, if it is all about me why should I worry about self-discipline in the first place—why not just do what I want when I want? This is the kind of attitude socialism encourages.

- *Responsibility and accountability.* Responsibility and accountability used to be hallmark American traits. President Harry Truman made the concepts part of America's lexicon with his famous slogan: "The buck stops here." Unfortunately, the buck no longer stops here for many Americans. Rather than accept responsibility, the more common approach has become to blame someone else. People are no longer shamed by having unpaid bills or unfulfilled obligations. In years past when Americans saw someone in trouble they would ask, "How can I help?" Now they are more likely to say, "I don't want to get involved." These days no matter how irresponsible people might be in their personal choices or actions, they can still find a way to blame someone else. In fact, aided and abetted by an out-of-control legal system Americans have turned avoiding responsibility into an industry. If you buy a cup of steaming hot coffee at a fast food-restaurant and carelessly spill it in your lap, you are not responsible. Blame the restaurant and sue. If you smoke cigarettes all your life and contract lung cancer, you are not responsible. Blame the cigarette manufacturer and sue. If you overeat all your life, never exercise, and have an obesity-induced heart attack, you are not responsible. Blame the grocery store and sue. "It's not my fault" has become a mantra in a country that used to say, "the buck stops here."

- *Deferred gratification.* There was a time before the days of no-interest loans and the ubiquitous credit card when Americans saved up for purchases they wanted to make but could not yet afford. To accommodate this thrifty approach, retailers invented the concept of layaway, and it served Americans well for decades. In addition, Americans used to believe patience is a virtue. But now 24/7/365 access coupled with the ability of computers, the internet, smart phones, microwave ovens, and other technologies to respond instantly has eliminated much of the perceived need to wait. Unfortunately, no matter how beneficial time-saving technologies may be, they also have a downside. A negative aspect of time-saving technologies is they contribute to a growing spirit of impatience that undermines the self-discipline needed to exercise deferred gratification. This impatience is showing up in detrimental ways to society (e.g., out-of-control credit spending, road rage, people answering cell phones at inappropriate times, customers demanding everything right now, people eating too many unhealthy fast-food meals, the stress created when people want others to respond immediately in the manner of computers, etc.). In American politics this cultural impatience shows up in demands for Congress to "do something" immediately rather than carefully consider proposed legislation; pass 1,000-page bills without reading them; spend trillions of dollars; and raise taxes to pay for the benefits of the unread legislation.

- *Hard work.* Historically, Americans have been among the hardest working people in the world. A positive work ethic—derived from religious beliefs—ensured that Americans of previous generations worked hard. Unfortunately, demanding work no longer appeals to many Americans. Many Americans of prime working age would rather stake their economic security on government entitlements and their dreams of living the good life on winning the lottery rather than working hard to succeed.

Working smart, which was originally intended to be a strategy for becoming more productive, is now viewed as a strategy for working less. The attitude of many Americans toward working these days is summarized in the following question: "Why should I work when the government will take care of me?" It is this attitude that created the unprecedented situation in 2021 wherein employers could not find people to work because potential employees were sitting home collecting government stipends under the misnamed American Rescue Act. Employers had to cut back on their hours and some even went out of business because the government paid potential employees to stay home.

The erosion of such traditional American values as thrift, diligence, self-reliance, self-discipline, responsibility, accountability, deferred gratification, and challenging work led to the types of behaviors threatening the long-term viability of America's economy. Consequently, only by restoring those values will Americans be able to continue to enjoy the quality of life to which they have become accustomed.

SOME WORK-ETHIC BASICS

The work ethic is what individuals and societies believe about work as a concept. These beliefs translate into their attitudes toward work. Is work good or bad? Is it delight or drudgery? Is it a blessing or curse? Should work be done only by lesser members of society or should all people work? Is work something to be actively sought or assiduously avoided? How people answer these questions is determined by their work ethic.

Over time, the views of individuals and societies concerning work have evolved. Ancient Hebrews thought of work as drudgery inflicted on them as punishment for the disobedience of Adam and Eve in the garden of Eden. Ancient Greeks also viewed work with a jaundiced eye. They saw it as something to be done by slaves, not by gentlemen. Philosophers such as Plato and Aristotle thought work interfered with the more important human endeavors such as music, philosophy, art, and literature. Romans, like the Greeks, thought of work as the domain of slaves; something they should avoid so as not to blur the line between master and minion.

During the Middle-Ages, attitudes toward work began to change, but only slightly. Instead of being viewed as something to be avoided, work took on a utilitarian aspect. Work was still viewed as lacking any intrinsic value, but it did become an accepted way of providing for a family and avoiding the need for charity. In other words, work was then perceived as having value but only in the utilitarian sense that it allowed man to independently provide for his daily bread. It still had no intrinsic value.

It was during the Protestant Reformation when the work-as-drudgery attitude began to change. Martin Luther and John Calvin contributed more than anyone to the new perspective on work now associated with the Protestant Reformation. As a result of the teachings of Luther and Calvin, Christian-dominated societies began to view work as being ordained for the glory of God and the fulfillment of God's purpose on earth. This, in turn, made it inherently good. A logical extension of this new perspective was to view working diligently to serve and honor God as well to thank him for the opportunity work provided to improve one's circumstances. This thankful, diligent attitude toward work crystallized into what eventually became known as the Protestant work ethic, although the first use of the term did not occur until much later.

The phrase "Protestant work ethic" was coined by German economist and sociologist, Max Weber, in his landmark book, *The Protestant Ethic and the Spirit of Capitalism* (1904 and 1905).[3] Weber attributed the advanced development, quality of life, and prosperity enjoyed by Western society to the positive work ethic of Christians.

The concept has also been called the Puritan work ethic by those who associate it with John Calvin's emphasis on arduous work as a Christian obligation and as evidence of salvation. Calvin professed those who are saved will show evidence of the fact through, among other things, their dedication to thrift, diligence, self-discipline, self-reliance, responsibility, accountability, delayed gratification, and hard work.

Work Ethic Defined

To understand the American version of the work ethic, it is necessary to first understand the Protestant work ethic as envisioned by Calvin. Calvin taught that diligence and dedication to doing a good job in one's work pleases God and is a form of worship.[4]

American Work Ethic

The American work ethic is a direct descendant of the Protestant work ethic. It is a peculiarly American mix of Christian values, rugged individualism, entrepreneurship, economic necessity, patriotism, and the need to compete to get ahead. This multifaceted version of the work ethic can be summarized as follows:

Work is good because it:

1. provides individuals with opportunities to achieve financial security, professional success, personal satisfaction, and material wealth;
2. affords individuals opportunities to contribute to society;
3. helps entrepreneurs who create jobs achieve maximum competitiveness through peak performance and continual improvement, and
4. helps America maintain its freedom and position of leadership in the world.

Consequently, people should approach work with an attitude of thrift, diligence, self-reliance, self-discipline, responsibility, accountability, and deferred gratification. Further, people should take pride in working hard and in doing an excellent job no matter what their job may be.

The Protestant work ethic played a critical role in the development of the American colonies and the establishment of the United States. As our nation grew, the work ethic played a critical role in the achievement of manifest destiny and the eventual establishment of America as an economic superpower.

America is now the last great bastion of freedom in the world, but it is also a nation whose freedom is threatened from within by a growing entitlement mentality fast replacing the ambitious spirit and traditional work ethic. America's ability to maintain its position of leadership in the world is based in large measure on the ability of individual Americans and businesses to out-think, out-work, and out-perform the competition in the global arena. Outperforming global competition at the individual and organizational levels requires an entrepreneurial spirit and positive work ethic.

WHY THE WORK ETHIC IS SO IMPORTANT IN TODAY'S GLOBAL WORLD

A nation's quality of life in the age of globalization is determined in large measure by the competitiveness of its private sector. The competitiveness of the private sector is determined by many factors, but none more than the performance of individual businesses. The performance of a business, in turn, is a function of the performance of its personnel, and few things affect the performance of people more than their work ethic. Of course, knowledge and skills are critical elements of human performance, but unless they are energized by a positive work ethic, knowledge and skills are just idle assets.

A nation's work ethic is a major determiner of its ability to compete in the global marketplace. Correspondingly, a nation's ability to compete in the global marketplace is a major determiner of its quality of life. It follows from this that a declining work ethic will result in a declining quality of life. This is the situation currently confronting America. Rather than encouraging entrepreneurship, individual initiative, and self-reliance, the government is adopting socialist policies that undermine the work ethic, provide bailouts, handouts, and entitlements; and result in burdensome regulations and oppressive centralized controls.

THE WORK ETHIC'S EFFECT ON OTHER ASPECTS OF LIFE

America has become like a large wagon in which too many people are riding and too few are pulling. Those riding in the wagon have lost their work ethic or, more likely, never developed one in the first place. The traditional work ethic is important to our country because it affects all aspects of a person's life, not just the work related aspects. An individual's work ethic is part of a broader worldview that determines how he or she lives every aspect of life.

Individuals with a positive work ethic will conduct their lives much differently than those who think they are entitled to whatever they want whenever they want with someone else paying for it. A positive work ethic applies to all aspects of an individual's life. Unfortunately, so does an entitlement mentality. Further, just as the entrepreneurial spirit and traditional work ethic complement each other in ways beneficial to society, socialism and the entitlement mentality reinforce each other in detrimental ways.

People with a positive work ethic apply its various elements to all aspects of their lives. It is important to grasp this point if America is going to turn its back on socialism and say no to the entitlement mentality. Individuals with a positive work ethic view the problems they face daily differently than those who have an entitlement mentality. Consider the issue of pursuing a college education. A person with a positive work ethic who wants to go to college but cannot afford it will think: "I am going to have to find a job that will allow me to work my way through college." A person with an entitlement mentality will think: "I need to apply for federal financial aid and government-backed student loans." The former sees paying for college as his responsibility, the latter thinks someone else should pay for it. That someone else, of course, is the American taxpayer.

People who lack a positive work ethic—those with an entitlement mentality—approach life from the perspective of what someone else can do for them because they think they are entitled. An individual with an entitlement mentality feels no shame in failing to pay bills or make good on promises. Why worry about these things when your perspective on life can be summarized in just three words: *I am entitled.* People who have an entitlement mentality are takers. They feel entitled to ride in the economic wagon. People who have a positive work ethic are contributors. They know the wagon must be pulled and feel responsible for helping pull it.

The entitlement mentality is a critical factor contributing to our country's courtship with socialism. Hence, the entitlement mentality must be eliminated and replaced by the ambitious spirit and traditional work ethic if America is going to stop the current downhill slide toward socialism. You do not cure a drug addict by giving him more drugs or an alcoholic by giving him drinks. Reward irresponsibility and sloth, and you will get more of the same. This is precisely what socialism does and it is why government bailouts, handouts, and entitlements are detrimental to America's economy.

ENTITLEMENT MENTALITY AND THE "ME GENERATION"

The Me Generation consists of people born after the mid-1970s. Although individuals of all ages can develop an entitlement mentality, members of the Me Generation have been more prone to do so than previous generations. Unlike their predecessors, Me-Geners were raised in circumstances encouraging the development of an entitlement mentality. Overindulgent parents, the self-esteem movement, the teaching of socialist dogma in education, and the pandering it's-all-about-you message of ad campaigns and commercials have had a powerful effect on the attitudes of young people.

If during your formative years someone provided for your every want and whim while requiring nothing of you, it is reasonable to assume you might have developed an entitlement mentality. When children who are overindulged throughout their formative years become adults, the transition from depending on parents to depending on the government is a logical step. This transfer of dependence from parents to the government has been the pattern for Me-Geners.

These folks were given advantages their parents never had but were required to contribute nothing to their family's well-being. Brought up in an environment in which they were protected from the realities of life, told repeatedly how special they are, and given every material advantage, Me-Geners came to believe they deserved everything they want or need. They grew accustomed to the material comfort their parents provided and eventually learned to take it for granted. Little wonder then that the entrepreneurial spirit and traditional American work ethic have been replaced by an entitlement mentality in so many Americans. To make matters even worse, what overindulgent parents started, the government reinforces through handouts and other socialist programs.

As it gained a foothold in American culture, the entitlement mentality began to manifest itself in a variety of ways. Young people who thought they deserved material success and wanted it right now started consuming and accumulating based on easy credit. To make matters worse, the entitlement mentality began to have a detrimental effect on productivity. While Americans have been supersizing their lives and living beyond their means, productivity in the workplace has declined.

Beginning in the late 1980s, America's productivity began a downward trend and could no longer keep pace with competing industrialized nations such as Japan and South Korea. For example, Japanese automobile manufacturers require an average of fifteen hours to produce one new car. U.S. manufacturers require an average of twenty hours. When American automobile manufacturers must pay their unionized workforce higher wages and better benefits than their Japanese and Korean competitors, taking longer to produce a car puts the American companies at a competitive disadvantage.

By the time the first crop of Me-Geners became adults, they had grown accustomed to being indulged by parents and Leftist ideologues masquerading as teachers. Consequently, as adults—out of the nest and on their own—Me-Geners faced a dilemma: Who would take care of them now? The obvious answer was a ready-and-willing federal government controlled by Socialists only too eager to gain control over individuals by making them dependent. Adult Me-Geners began to view the government in the same way they always viewed their parents—as an omnipresent provider there to indulge their appetites and rescue them from their own irresponsibility and bad choices.

As Me-Geners came of voting age, there were plenty of pandering politicians willing to indulge the entitlement mentality of this new voting bloc, and none more skillfully than the Socialists who have gained a controlling foothold in the Democrat Party. Leftist politicians use the federal treasury to buy voter loyalty and

encourage voter dependency. They have taken to heart the words
of noted socialist George Bernard Shaw who said: "A government
which robs Peter to pay Paul can always count on Paul's support."[5]

ULTIMATE CONSEQUENCES OF SOCIALISM AND ENTITLEMENT IN AMERICA

Unfortunately, a declining quality of life is not the worst of what
Americans face in the twenty-first century if capitalism, the enterprising spirit, and the work ethic are not restored. The even greater
threat is to our freedom and liberty. In a world where the "hate
America" crowd is growing steadily in both influence and power,
our ability to maintain economic, military, and moral superiority
has never been more critical or more at risk. America's ability to
retain its historical position of global leadership is a function of
numerous intertwined and mutually dependent factors, one of the
more important of which is our nation's work ethic.

In today's hyper-competitive global marketplace, consistent
peak performance and continual improvement of performance
are organizational imperatives for commercial enterprises. Consequently, more than ever, employers need an entrepreneurial
spirit and need their personnel to have a positive work ethic. In
fact, only by restoring the work ethic can America hope to regain
the market losses it has incurred over the last three decades to
Japan, Korea, India, and China in some of our most critical commercial sectors.

As commercial enterprises in other industrialized nations continue to whittle away at the markets of American companies, the
quality of life in the United States is gradually eroding and the
freedoms we have historically enjoyed are increasingly at risk.
Whereas the United States historically maintained its quality of life
through unrivaled productivity, we are now depending on the socialist propensity for out-of-control borrowing. The United States is
like a family, once well off, is now forced to use credit cards to
maintain its standard of living. Such an approach can lead only to
insolvency, and sooner rather than later.

The relationship between a nation's entrepreneurial spirit and
work ethic and its freedom and liberty is clear and compelling. The

less competitive a nation, the more debt it is forced to incur. The more debt a nation incurs, the more it becomes a slave to lender nations, which is what is happening to America. What makes it even worse is the nations lending the most money to the United States are not respecters of freedom and liberty, nor do they have the best interests of America at heart.

Moreover, the military power essential to protect America against its enemies depends on our nations' wealth and technological superiority. Socialism will eventually destroy that wealth and technological superiority. Therefore, rejecting socialism and restoring capitalism, the entrepreneurial spirit, and the traditional work ethic in America are critically important commitments.

WHAT AMERICANS THINK ABOUT SOCIALISM: THE UGLY TRUTH

In a nation that built the strongest economy in the history of the world based on capitalism, entrepreneurship, and a positive work ethic, one would think socialism would be anathema. Unfortunately, this is not the case. In a Gallup poll, respondents were asked for their views concerning capitalism versus socialism. Those who chose capitalism were in the majority, but just barely (53 percent).[6] This means that in America—the land of freedom and opportunity—47 percent of our citizens now either prefer socialism or just do not know which system they prefer. Either way, this is a disturbing result.

The most disturbing aspect of the Gallup poll is how divided adults under thirty years of age are over the question of socialism versus capitalism. The Me Generation cannot be depended on to preserve the worldview and economic system that made America the most powerful nation in the world. Many Me-Geners prefer a system that has a long and consistent record of failure—socialism.

According to the Gallup poll, adults under the age of thirty responded to the question as follows: 37 percent prefer capitalism, 33 percent prefer socialism, and 30 percent are undecided.[7] This is a formal accusation of America's education system, mass media, entertainment industry, colleges, and universities and, to a certain extent, the church. It is something all Americans who want to save our country from socialist ideologues must come together to remedy.

Eberle summarizes his thoughts on America's turn toward socialism as follows:

> We are at a crossroads, and we must fight to get America back on track. The American way is not an effortless way. No one ever said it was. It is not about what the government can give you. The government cannot give a person anything it does not first take away from someone else. No person is entitled to what another person earns. The American way is about respecting the rights of the individual and promoting an economic and political system that provides opportunity for all.[8]

WHAT YOU CAN DO TO PRESERVE CAPITALISM AND REJECT SOCIALISM

Americans who want to save our country from those trying to destroy it must come together with one voice and say "no" to the socialist agenda being pushed by Leftist ideologues. Here are some specific things you and other American patriots can do to stop the socialist onslaught in its tracks:[9]

- Acknowledge God, not government, as the source of the rights Americans have long enjoyed.
- Advocate for limited government.
- Support initiatives to reduce regulations and taxation.
- Demand your constitutional rights be honored and protected.
- Demand elected officials rebuild the public school system and higher education based on traditional American values and weed out socialist ideologues.
- Promote the Christian work ethic over the entitlement mentality by demanding elected officials eliminate government handouts to idle people who should be working.
- Support Senators and federal judges who will protect the sovereignty and integrity of the Constitution.
- Support law and order and the police officers who try to maintain it.

- Demand state legislatures take the steps necessary to ensure fair and transparent elections in which only legal votes are counted and counted on time.

In his book *Vietnam, Now*, distinguished reporter David Lamb explains how free-market capitalism has shunted socialism aside in favor of capitalism by comparing the vibrant, economically bustling Ho Chi Minh City (formerly Saigon) with the drab idleness of Hanoi, seat of the country's communist government.[10] According to Lamb,

> The marriage of communism and capitalism was an odd one, and anyone who thinks communism is the stronger partner is naïve. . . . The North had won the war, but the South was winning the peace. . . . The Old Guard communist leadership of the North can bury its head in the sands of Marxist economic theory all it wants, but its constituency wants the model that Saigon symbolized—an economy that rewards initiative, encourages private enterprise, values liberal ideas, and frees itself from rigid government control.[11]

What happened in post-war Vietnam—one more nation where socialism failed—is what eventually happens in all socialist nations: the economy falters, chronic shortages become a way of life, and the government must turn to capitalism to save the nation from starvation. China's communist government has survived in the same way Viet Nam's government has survived: by loosening government control and allowing free enterprise to rescue its economy. It is not likely this odd mix of political and economic philosophies an endure forever. The eventual winner will be free enterprise, the loser socialism. These examples demonstrate once again why it is so important for American patriots to reject socialism and preserve capitalism.

CHAPTER 6

RESTORING PATRIOTISM AND LOVE OF COUNTRY

We grew up in an era when citizens of all ages loved the United States, were proud to be Americans, and believed in patriotism. In fact, love of one's country and a willingness to sacrifice for it is the definition of patriotism. As youngsters, we began every school day with the Pledge of Allegiance, and every classroom proudly displayed an American flag. Even first graders knew the words to our National Anthem. We stood tall with our right hands over our hearts as we sang the hallowed song.

Veterans were considered heroes; they were treated with respect and honored with parades on November 11 every year. Memorial Day saw families placing wreaths on the graves of family members, friends, and community members they did not even know who died in World War I, World War II, or the Korean War. But this all began to change in the 1960s. Respect for the flag was replaced with desecration of the flag. Patriots were jeered at and called jingoists or warmongers. Love of country was supplanted by disdain for the United States.

Fast-forward to the present. The seeds of anti-Americanism sown in the 1960s have grown into full-fledged WOKEISM in the twenty-first century. As a gesture of disrespect for a country they claim is inherently unfair and racist, highly paid athletes in the

National Football League (NFL) kneel when the National Anthem
is played rather than stand. Olympic athletes who wear the American flag on their jerseys kneel when the National Anthem is played
and turn their backs when the American flag is raised on the medal
platform. In just sixty-plus years, we evolved from a nation of patriots into a nation of ungrateful snowflakes who blame America for
all the ills of the world.

WOKEISM: THE ENEMY OF PATRIOTISM

WOKEISM is a view of the world based on outrage at perceived
social inequities, although much of the outrage is manufactured,
amounting to little more than outrage for the sake of outrage. This
artificial outrage is encouraged by Leftist ideologues in education,
business, industry, the entertainment industry, and even the military
to perpetuate social discord. This is another example of semantic
subterfuge. WOKEISM is a living nightmare, not an awakening.

WOKEISM is an easy concept to "sell" because it gives people
who have done nothing to improve their lives an excuse for their
circumstances and someone else to blame for their own shortcom-
ing. This is unfortunate because the worst thing you can do for
individuals who want to improve their lives is give them an excuse
for failing to do so. Originally envisioned as a movement to reject
oppression of minorities, opportunistic Leftists have transformed
WOKEISM into an instrument of oppression that does nothing to
help minorities.

In more practical terms, WOKEISM has evolved into a point
of view portraying America as a racist nation, white people as perpetual oppressors, and minorities as perpetual victims. To
WOKEISM advocates, being offended has replaced baseball as the
national pastime. To them, anything failing to toe the line of Leftist orthodoxy is considered offensive. To be politically correct in
the eyes of these Socialists and to be tolerated by them, you must
agree with them on all issues. There is no room in a Leftist's mind
for counterargument or dissent.

A particularly destructive aspect of WOKEISM is identity politics wherein Americans are divided by race, sexual orientation, and

any other factor the Left can use to separate them into tribal groups. This is the Democrats' divide-and-conquer strategy. Because of this aspect of WOKEISM, E Pluribus Unum has been replaced by tribalism, and the concept of united we stand has been replaced by an us-against-them attitude.

Because the Socialists control education at all levels in much of America, WOKEISM is what children are being taught in the K–12 system and young adults are being taught in colleges and universities. Six-year-old white children are being taught their parents are evil oppressors and they themselves will grow up to be oppressors. Six-year-old minority children are being taught they are perpetual victims with no chance in life (without government help). Young people in public school and colleges are also being taught white people who never owned slaves should be forced to pay reparations to black people who have never been slaves.

Based on the Left's claim of perpetual victimhood, WOKEISTS believe wealth and property should be divided up on the basis of race rather than merit with no regard for individual performance, effort, character, or relative contributions to society. This is the redistribution of wealth principle of WOKEISM. Apply the affirmative action principal of Socialists to the National Basketball Association (NBA) where 74 percent of the players are black and only 17 percent are white and the racial breakdown would become: Black-13 percent, White-76 percent, Asian-6 percent, Indian/Alaskan native-1.3 percent, and other 3.7 percent. The Left's redistribution-of-wealth principle would drive the NBA out of business in a week. The same is true of what will happen when this principle is applied to America's economy.

If the Left's claim that people of color are perpetual victims who have no chance of bettering their lots in life is true, why require minority children to attend school in the first place? What good is it going to do them? Education has long been recognized as one of the key ingredients in building a better life. Millions of Americans of all races have bettered their lives using education as the springboard to success. The Socialists simply ignore this fact and teach minority children they are going to spend their lives as victims unless merit-based capitalism is replaced by race-based socialism.

Organizations such as Black Lives Matter (BLM) use WOKEISM to justify fomenting riots in which businesses are looted, property is destroyed, and innocent citizens are violently attacked. WOKEISM was the basis for the "defund the police" movement that sprang up in 2021 and quickly blew up in the face of its Democrat advocates. Claiming police officers are instruments of oppression, Leftist officials in several large cities defunded their police departments only to have violent crime skyrocket overnight.

Fortunately, common sense has prevailed in some cases and several of those cities have begun to quietly *re-fund* their police departments. That is the good news. The bad news is few people want to serve as police officers in cities with records of supporting criminal behavior rather than law and order. Consequently, rebuilding police departments in Leftist-controlled cities is going to be a challenge, a fact very encouraging to criminals in those cities.

Leftist ideologues intent on destroying the United States were quick to realize they could use WOKEISM to their advantage. They have endeavored to weaponize the concept and use it as one more strategy for attacking God and country. To weaponize WOKEISM, Democrats use it as the basis for character assassination, personal destruction, the cancel culture, fomenting racial discord, and portraying America as an evil empire. Its targets, of course, are patriots who still believe in the America of the Founders and our national symbols, particularly the American flag and our National Anthem.

WOKEISM and NFL Players Kneeling During the National Anthem

National Football League (NFL) players kneeling during the National Anthem is a quintessential example of the hypocrisy and idiocy of WOKEISM. Players who kneel during the National Anthem claim they do so because the United States is an inherently unfair country where minorities have no chance to succeed. Bear in mind the least paid player in the NFL—one who sits on the bench and never gets into the game—is paid more than $400,000 per year regardless his race. NFL stars make millions.

By kneeling they claim to be ashamed of America because the lingering effects of slavery are sustaining the sins of racial inequality and unfairness to minorities. The players who kneel—excluding those who do so out of peer pressure—claim minorities are still just as oppressed as they were during the days of slavery. They also claim whites are inherently oppressive, oppressing minorities is in their DNA.

The worst aspect of seeing NFL players showing disrespect to our national symbols is knowing young children are watching their football heroes and will imitate their actions. Whether they want to be or not, professional athletes are role models for youngsters. They have a powerful influence over what youngsters come to believe and how they choose to behave. This, of course, is precisely why the Left supported the NFL kneeling phenomenon.

Colin Kaepernick of the San Francisco 49ers is the player most strongly associated with the kneeling phenomenon in the National Football League (NFL). He began kneeling during the National Anthem in September 2016. At the time he was a second-string quarterback who earned $35 million dollars in three years with the San Francisco 49ers for sitting on the bench. How ironic is it a black man earning $35 million for sitting on his backside and watching his team play football would claim minorities like him have no chance of succeeding in America?

It was blatant hubris and hypocrisy for Kaepernick and other minority players in the NFL to kneel in protest of the inequities of American society when the people watching them from the stands—most of them white—were mostly living from paycheck to paycheck, splurging to watch the game. The real inequity is the interest on $35 million dollars for just one year amounted to more than most Americans earn after working for twenty-five years.

To show how out of touch Leftist ideologues are with the American public, the kneeling phenomenon was so unpopular with fans, NFL revenue plummeted. The more players knelt during the National Anthem, the fewer fans showed up for games or watched on television. NFL fans viewed kneeling during the National Anthem as a sign of disrespect for military personnel—active and veterans—as well as their families.

Leftist ideologues pushing the kneeling phenomenon finally went too far when NFL players choose to kneel during the National

Anthem on National Gold Star Mother's Day. This special day pays tribute to the mothers of America's soldiers, sailors, airmen, guardsman, and Marines killed in combat. Imagine how difficult it must have been for grieving mothers to see or hear about overpaid NFL players disrespecting the anthem and flag their children died fighting for. The blatant insensitivity required to disrespect the flag on such a hallowed, grief-filled day is difficult to comprehend.

This incredibly callous act undermined the validity of their cause in the eyes of many Americans. Kneeling players were suddenly viewed as not just unpatriotic ingrates, they were seen as hardhearted, uncaring, unappreciative whiners.

Embarrassed, some players claimed they were unaware of the day. Being unaware of Gold Star Mother's Day and its significance is no excuse. If players did not know, they should have. If those who did not know were not so blinded by their own self-righteousness victimhood, they would have known. Those who knew about the day and still knelt were even worse. Theirs was a contemptible act of monumental self-centeredness.

Reprehensible acts such as kneeling during the National Anthem on Gold Star Mother's Day finally threw a wet blanket on Colin Kaepernick and company. The kneeling phenomenon began to fizzle except for a few hard-core ingrates and their weak teammates who succumbed to peer pressure and went along to get along. However, this was not the end of the Left's war on America and its national symbols. Fast-forward to the present. As the NFL kneeling phenomenon began to wane, it was given new life by some of America's Olympic athletes.

Olympic Athletes Disrespect America's Flag and National Anthem

The kneeling phenomenon eventually became a loser for the NFL and players began to feel pressured by owners, coaches, and even their peers to find a more appropriate way to express their manufactured outrage. What they eventually settled on was still offensive and divisive. More about that in the next section of this chapter.

At the same time the NFL was moving past the kneeling phenomenon, some of America's elite Olympic athletes picked up the ball and ran with it. Kneeling during the National Anthem, turning their backs on the American flag when it was raised on the medal stand, and refusing to march behind the flag during the opening ceremony became commonplace for some of America's Olympic athletes.

Many Americans viewed these gestures by Olympians as even more disrespectful than NFL players kneeling. While NFL players represent a city—Dallas Cowboys, Cincinnati Bengals, Atlanta Falcons, etc.—Olympians represent the United States of America and wear the American flag on their jerseys. Worse yet, while the NFL players knelt before a mostly American audience, Olympic athletes showed their disrespect for our country (and theirs) on an international stage before the eyes of the world. Many Americans were so offended by the disrespect some of our Olympic athletes showed the flag and the National Anthem that they rooted for the teams and athletes of other countries.

During the 2021 Olympics two American athletes created controversy by purposefully disrespecting the American flag. Their protests generated a tidal wave of negative feedback for both. During the Olympic trials, hammer thrower, Gwen Berry, won a bronze medal. On the medal stand, Berry turned her back on the American flag and held up a shirt that read "Activist Athlete." Her gesture resulted in demands she be disqualified and removed from the U.S. Olympic team. However, the controversy over her disrespectful gesture soon died out when she turned out to be a better activist than athlete. During the Olympic finals she placed eleventh out of twelve hammer throwers.

Megan Rapinoe already had a reputation for disrespecting the American flag and National Anthem before the 2021 Olympic Games. In fact, many Americans viewed Rapinoe as the "Colin Kaepernick" of women's soccer. Her anti-American protests began in September 2016. At first, she protested by refusing to place her hand over her heart during the National Anthem. Kneeling during the National Anthem came later.

When asked why she refused to place her hand over her heart during the National Anthem, Rapinoe responded she would never put her hand over her heart or sing the National Anthem. She tried to deflect criticism by claiming her protests were aimed more at Donald Trump than the United States, but that explanation fell flat when it was pointed out her protests began before Trump was elected.[1] Her credibility concerning why she refused to honor the flag was further damaged when she not only knelt during the 2021 Olympics but was accused of pressuring teammates to kneel.[2]

As happened with Gwen Berry, the controversy surrounding Rapinoe's protest during the 2021 Olympics quickly died out when the American team failed to win gold as was expected and had to settle for a bronze medal. Americans had lofty expectations for the women's Olympic soccer team, so the bronze medal felt like a loss. Berry and Rapinoe soon learned Americans are more open to hearing the protests of winners than losers.

Leftist ideologues were more disappointed by Berry's loss and the women soccer team's bronze medal than anyone else because they want young children to be influenced by their Olympic heroes. When the media quickly lost interest in the Berry and Rapinoe protests and focused more on their disappointing showings, the Left lost an opportunity that comes along only every four years. Their cause was hurt even more when American Olympic athletes who won their events proudly carried the American flag on their victory laps.

Playing the "Black National Anthem" at NFL Games

We mentioned earlier that when the kneeling phenomenon lost steam, the NFL found a way to appease—read *pander to*—the disgruntled Leftist players who still want to show their disdain for America and its national symbols. In fact, the NFL is becoming more about the Leftist social justice movement than about football. The NFL's latest Leftist ploy is playing the "Black National Anthem" before games, the hymn "Lift Every Voice and Sing."

"Lift Every Voice and Sing" was written as a poem by civil rights activist, James Weldon Johnson. Johnson's brother, a composer, set the poem to music in 1919 and the NAACP soon adopted it as the "Negro National Anthem."[3] "Lift Every Voice and Sing" is a powerful song about the journey from slavery to the promised land, a

song well-known to Christians of all races. Considering the circumstances in some parts of America in 1919, one can understand why
black Americans would want their own anthem back then. America
was a different country in 1919 than it is today. Much has changed
in America since 1919, and the changes have been for the better
when it comes to racial equality.

The NFL was founded in 1920 soon after the NAACP adopted
"Lift Every Voice and Sing" as its anthem. Fritz Pollard, star running back from Brown University, became its first black player.
Despite his pioneering efforts the number of black players in the
NFL remained small for some time. However, the challenging work
of civil rights leaders, black and white, changed this situation. As of
2021, 60 percent of players in the NFL are black.[4] To put this figure
in perspective, 12.4 percent of Americans are black.

Progress toward racial equality has been achieved because people of good will of all races sought to come together around shared
values, dreams, ambitions, and principles. The NAACP and leaders
of the civil rights movement sought equality of the races, not division. The identity politics and tribalism pushed by Democrats was
what civil rights leaders sought to eliminate. They abhorred separation of the races—segregation—and fought long and hard to
eliminate it. Having a separate anthem for black Americans is a
strategy for re-segregation, which is precisely what Leftist ideologues want. It is just one more tactic in their overall strategy of
divide and conquer.

The hypocrisy of the NFL in playing the "Black National
Anthem" before games is blatant. It is the result of executives who
are interested only in ticket sales and television ratings pandering
to Leftist ideologues in hopes of avoiding the controversy they
might stir up and boycotts they might call for. If the NFL commis-
sioner and team owners were that interested in improving black
lives, they would stop their hypocritical pandering and start working
to reduce violent crime and improve living conditions in the neigh-
borhoods many of their players came from.

Armstrong Williams calls the NFL's attempts at placating Democrats "dressed-up symbolism" and "progressive white wokeness,"
neither of which does anything to improve the lives of black

Americans. He rightly claims if the NFL genuinely wants to do something to help improve the lives of black Americans, they should invest in after-school tutoring and mentoring programs to help black youngsters improve their academic skills. "They should focus on guiding young boys to become better men, and young girls to become strong, independent women."[5]

WOKEISM is about sowing seeds of discord, dividing Americans by skin color, pitting the races against each other, encouraging tribalism, and teaching young people to hate our country. It is the opposite of the American ideal of E Pluribus Unum. The traditional melting-pot concept is critical in a nation as diverse and pluralistic as the United States.

Diversity is one of the defining characteristics of the United States. The ancestors of many Americans came from every other country in the world. Traditionally, this land of immigrants came together as one (E Pluribus Unum) by focusing on shared values, principles, ambitions, and dreams—not race, gender, or identity. It has always been these shared values and the freedom to pursue their dreams that caused Americans of all races and national origins to love our country. To restore patriotism and love of country, we must once again focus on the things Americans of different races have in common and reject the Left's efforts to divide and conquer by focusing on and even creating differences.

WHAT YOU CAN DO TO RESTORE PATRIOTISM AND LOVE OF COUNTRY

WOKEISM is the opposite of patriotism. Rather than encourage love of country and E Pluribus Unum, WOKEISM encourages an I-hate-America mentality, racial discord, and tribalism. This being the case, what can Americans who want to restore the vision of our Founders do? How can we restore the patriotism and love of country that were once the norm in America?

Writing for *Daedalus*, Jeffrey Mirel answers this question as follows: "To start reversing the deconstruction of Americanism, we need a concerted counter-revolution, one in which traditional American common sense is elevated above grievance-mongering and tribalist point-scoring."[6] The counter-revolution Mirel writes about is not a top-down movement from Washington, DC. Rather, it must be a bottom-up effort beginning at the local level with individual American patriots coming together in a united front against the anti-American machinations of the Left. What follows in the remainder of this chapter are specific things you and other individual Americans can do to restore patriotism and love of country.

Understand What Patriotism Is and What It Is Not

Patriotism is love of country, but not as a geographical location on a map. It is love of the ideals that define a country. Our Founders were clear concerning what these defining ideals were for America. They include individual rights that come from God—not man—personal liberty, popular sovereignty, republicanism, limited government, equality, opportunity, and personal responsibility. We love America because we love these ideals.

Unfortunately, patriotism is in decline in America, particularly among younger citizens—the ones who have been indoctrinated by Leftist ideologues in the K–12 system and colleges and universities. A Gallup poll released in 2021 found . . . that the share of participants who felt 'extremely proud' to be Americans was the lowest in the poll's 18-year history—just 47%, down from 70% in 2003 . . . the younger you are, the less likely you are to say that patriotism is a 'very important' value."[7]

Patriotism is not nationalism, although the two terms are often used interchangeably. Nationalism is support for the interests of one's country based on practical considerations rather than defining ideals. The problem with nationalism is it can get out of hand and become excessive. This happens when the interests of a given country are pursued to the detriment of other countries. Leftists accused President Donald Trump of this form of nationalism when he made "America First" part of his political platform. But they missed a crucial point.

When President Trump pursued an America First agenda he was simply reversing the nationalism other countries practiced to the detriment of the United States, like China. Protecting your

country's interests against other countries running roughshod over
them is not nationalism; it is good foreign policy.

Patriotism is love of country. Nationalism is support for the best
interests of one's country. There is nothing wrong with nationalism
unless it is pursued to an extreme as China and Russia are doing,
but it is patriotism—not nationalism—that makes people willing to
fight and die for our country. It is patriotism that makes Americans
proud to be Americans. Therefore, one of the goals of this book is
to restore patriotism and love of country.

Take Control of Public Education

The reason so many younger Americans do not love our country is
simple: they have been taught by Leftist ideologues masquerading
as teachers to hate the United States. A whole generation of young
people have been thoroughly indoctrinated in our public schools to
view America as a country unworthy of their love or respect, a nation
founded for the sole purpose of perpetuating slavery, a nation in
which white people are genetically programmed to be oppressors
and minorities are perpetual victims. Therefore, we will never
restore love of country until we take control of the public schools
in our local communities.

While this might sound like a monumental task, it does not have
to be. Leftist ideologues were able to gain control of America's
educational institutions because patriots were asleep at the switch,
we were not paying attention. When it comes to the public K–12
system, you—the American taxpayer—are the owners. Your taxes
pay for the schools. Further, you elect school superintendents and
school board members. Local patriots have enormous power if they
are willing to exercise it.

All that is necessary to take control of public education is for
patriots to come together and exercise their power. As of this writing, concerned mothers and fathers in local communities all over
America are speaking up at school board meetings, demanding truth
in education and the elimination of Critical Race Theory (CRT)
from the curriculum. Some are pulling their children out of the
public schools and enrolling them in Christian schools, private

schools, or homeschooling them. This is a particularly effective strategy because declining enrollments get the attention of school boards faster than almost any other factor. Declining enrollments result in a corresponding decline in funding.

Although it is important for patriots to speak up at school board meetings and to closely monitor what is being taught in the public schools, these things are not enough. We need to serve on PTAs where we can monitor the curriculum, textbook selection, and teaching methods. We need to run for school board seats. We also need to run for school superintendent or support other patriots who do. Patriots who want to save our country must be as engaged and as zealous as the Socialists who want to destroy it. Finally, we need to demand that state legislatures require the teaching of civics and true, unaltered American history.

We also need to demand that state legislatures curb the power of teachers' unions. Teachers' unions control public education and Leftist ideologues control teachers' unions. Teachers' unions show little or no concern for the quality of education provided at the local level. Their interests lie in demanding ever-increasing levels of pay and benefits without any evidence of improved performance, less interaction with students, more time off, and advancing their Leftist agenda.

Honor Active Duty Military Personnel, Veterans, and Their Families

Leftist teachers and textbooks portray military personnel and veterans as "aggressive hawks" and "warmongers" deserving only of disdain. To counter this portrayal, it is critical that patriots honor military personnel, veterans, and their families and teach their children and grandchildren to do so. If your community holds special tribute events on Memorial Day (last Monday in May), Veterans Day (November 11), Wreaths Across America Day (held the Saturday before Christmas each year), and National Gold Star Mother's Day (last Sunday in September), participate in these events and have your children and grandchildren participate with you.

Too many Americans view Memorial Day and Veterans Day as nothing more than a day off from work and an opportunity for a cookout. If your community does not hold tribute events on these special days, gather a group of fellow patriots and organize the events yourself. Involve your children and grandchildren in the planning and execution of the events. Explain the significance of these special days to them and why it is important to honor active duty military personnel, veterans, and their families.

Do not rely on anyone else to counter the lies of the Left. Make teaching your children and grandchildren to honor those who serve and have served and their families a do-it-yourself project. Reach out to veterans in your community and thank them for their service. Ask them to share why they served with your children and grandchildren. Let your children and grandchildren see firsthand that veterans are heroes not "warmongers."

Support Law Enforcement Officers and Firefighters

In addition to honoring military personnel, veterans, and their families, it is important to support those who put their lives on the line every day in your community. Support law enforcement officers and firefighters. If you live in a community governed by feckless Democrat officials who want to defund the police, stand up and speak out against this travesty. Support only political candidates who support the police and work hard to unseat officials who do not.

Stop by your local fire station from time to time and say, "thank you." Take your children and grandchildren with you. Bring the firefighters a snack every now and then. If you see police officers or firefighters eating in a restaurant, stop by their table and say, "thank you." Pick up the tab for their meal if you can afford to. Make a point of letting them know you appreciate their service.

Display the Flag and Teach Your Children and Grandchildren the Pledge of Allegiance

People our age grew up reciting the Pledge of Allegiance first thing in the morning every school day. To this day, we know the words by heart. Unfortunately, schools run by Leftist ideologues no longer recite the Pledge of Allegiance. Consequently, many youngsters these days cannot recite the Pledge even if given a chance; they do not know the words. This is unacceptable.

Do not rely on schools or anyone else to instruct your children and grandchildren to recite the Pledge of Allegiance. Do it yourself. Display the American flag and begin each day by reciting the Pledge of Allegiance with your children: *"I pledge allegiance to the flag of the United States of America, and to the republic for which it stands, one nation under God, indivisible, with liberty and justice for all."* When you children and grandchildren are old enough to understand, explain the meaning and significance of such concepts from the Pledge as "allegiance," "republic," "one nation under God," "indivisible," "liberty," and "justice for all."

Teach Your Children and Grandchildren the National Anthem and What It Means

Just as schools run by Leftist ideologues no longer teach children the Pledge of Allegiance, they have also done away with singing the National Anthem. This is a travesty. Much to the delight of Socialists who want to destroy our country, a lot of young Americans cannot sing our country's National Anthem because they do not know the words. Worse yet, they do not know the meaning or significance of the words.

Our National Anthem is officially called "The Star-Spangled Banner," a reference to the American flag. Teach your children and grandchildren the story of how the National Anthem came into being. Teach them how an American attorney, Francis Scott Key, on board a British man-of-war to negotiate the release of patriot prisoners, was able to observe the horrific bombardment of Fort McHenry by the British armada in Baltimore Harbor during the War of 1812. When the British were unable to subdue the fort and the American flag was still proudly waving after the battle, Key was so moved he wrote a poem about the battle. That poem was eventually set to music, and on March 3, 1931, Congress adopted "The Star-Spangled Banner" as America's National Anthem.

Teach your children and grandchildren the fifty stars on the American flag represent the fifty states that make up the United States. The thirteen stripes represent the original thirteen colonies. The white stripes symbolize purity and innocence, the blue stripes symbolize valor and hardiness, and the blue background for the stars symbolizes justice, perseverance, and vigilance. Teach your children and grandchildren the meaning and significance of the closing words to the Anthem: ". . . land of the free and the home of the brave."

Do the things we recommend in this chapter, and you will go a long way toward restoring patriotism and love of country by creating a new generation of young patriots who will join the battle to save our country from Leftist ideologues who want to destroy it. This is crucial because reversing the course Democrats have charted for our country will be a multi-generational battle.

CHAPTER 7

OVERCOMING DOMESTIC THREATS TO THE END GAME

S teps in the blueprint for rescuing America from progressive Left-ist ideologues presented thus far include achieving a spiritual revival, preserving the Constitution and Bill of Rights, rejecting historical revisionism, refuting the lies of the Left, preserving capitalism while rejecting socialism, and restoring patriotism and love of country. To accomplish these steps, it will be necessary to overcome several specific domestic and foreign threats standing in the way. This chapter explains how to overcome the domestic threats that could derail the blueprint for saving America.

DOMESTIC THREATS TO THE END GAME THAT MUST BE OVERCOME

To save America's end game for the twenty-first century from Left-ist ideologues who want to destroy our country, patriots must over-come the following domestic threats:

- An out-of-control federal government
- An entitlement mentality that is replacing personal responsibility
- Greedy, unpatriotic corporate executives and technology czars
- A rising tide of anarchy undermining law and order
- WOKE military leadership and an unprepared military

- Illegal immigration at the southern border
- Attacks on the Constitution and Bill of Rights
- A broken education system at all levels
- Growing acceptance of socialism/communism
- A compromised election system

The last three threats on this list have been covered in detail in previous chapters of this book. What you can do to help overcome the remaining threats on the list is covered in this chapter.

OUT-OF-CONTROL GOVERNMENT

America's Founders would be aghast at how the federal government has grown beyond anything they ever envisioned. All three branches of government well exceed the limits prescribed for them in the Constitution. In this section, we demonstrate how oversized and unwieldly all three branches of the federal government have grown and what you can do to help bring the federal government under control and return it to the limits envisioned by the Founders.

Growth of the Executive Branch

The powers of the president as delineated in Article II, Section 2 of the U.S. Constitution include: 1) Serve as commander-in-chief of the military, 2) Make treaties with other countries, 3) Appoint ambassadors, public ministers, consuls, judges, and any other officers of the United States whose appointments are not provided for elsewhere in the Constitution; and 4) Fill vacancies that occur during a recess of the Senate.

Based on this delineation of constitutional powers and duties, the executive branch should consist of the Department of Defense, Department of State, Department of Justice, Treasury Department, and Executive Office of the President. The Founders who wrote the Constitution would be shocked to learn, as of this writing, the executive branch consists of the Executive Office of the President and a long list of extra-constitutional agencies, bureaus, commissions, and boards. Here is a list of just the departments. Bear in mind each of these departments consists of multiple subunits:

- Executive Office of the President (EOP)
- Department of Agriculture (USDA)
- Department of Commerce (DOC)
- Department of Defense (DOD)
- Department of Education (DOE)
- Department of Energy (DOE)
- Department of Health and Human Services (HHS)
- Department of Homeland Security (DHS)
- Department of Housing and Urban Development (HUD)
- Department of the Interior (DOI)
- Department of Justice (DOJ)
- Department of Labor (DOL)
- Department of State (DOS)
- Department of Transportation (DOT)
- Department of the Treasury
- Department of Veterans Affairs

In addition to these departments and their numerous subunits, the executive branch also includes sixty agencies, bureaus, commissions, foundations, boards, and advisory councils. These include the Central Intelligence Agency (CIA), Federal Deposit Insurance Corporation, National Endowment for the Arts, National Science Foundation, Tennessee Valley Authority, Financial Protection Bureau, Board of Governors of the Federal Reserve, Federal Maritime Commission, National Labor Relations Board, Equal Employment Opportunity Commission, Selective Service System, and National Transportation and Safety Board to name just a few examples.

It is next to impossible for a president of the United States to even remember all the departments, agencies, boards, commissions, bureaus, foundations, and advisory councils under the executive branch much less efficiently and effectively manage them. Even considering the growth of our country and the international circumstances existing today that did not exist when the Constitution was ratified in 1788, the executive branch of government far exceeds the limits prescribed for it in the Constitution.

To make matters worse, many of the agencies bloating the executive branch issue burdensome regulations. Of the four million people who work in the various departments, agencies, and bureaus, only two are elected by the people: the president and vice president. Unelected bureaucrats wield enormous power over businesses and the lives of individual American citizens who have no say in selecting them and can do little or nothing about having them removed.

These bureaucrats promulgate federal regulations prescribing how American citizens work and live. Rather than being the government of the people envisioned by the Founders, we have become a government operating for the sake of the elected officials and bureaucrats in government rather than the governed.

Federal regulations are supposed to translate the laws passed by Congress into practical language to eliminate ambiguities in the laws. But this is not what happens. Rather than just translate laws into practical language, regulations often add to and even multiply their effects. The number of regulations promulgated by federal government bureaucrats every year far surpasses the number of laws passed by our elected officials in Congress by a ratio of twenty-seven to one.[1] The compliance costs regulations generate add 20 percent to the cost of doing business in America and this does not include the unintended costs that often exceed the known compliance costs.[2]

Growth of the Legislative Branch

The growth of the Legislative Branch comes from the number of bureaucrats that members of the House and Senate are allotted to staff their offices as well as their committees and subcommittees. The House and Senate combined maintain 250 committees, all of which are staffed by bureaucrats paid for by the American taxpayer. There are 435 members of the House and Senate, and each member is allotted a team of tax-supported staff members. A senator's staff can range in size from twenty to sixty members while congresspeople are authorized staffs of eighteen full-time personnel and four part-time. Staff sizes have grown steadily over the years, peaking in 1977 at 6,556 congressional staff members. In 2021 the number was slightly lower at 6,329.[3]

That is a lot of bureaucrats on the federal tax rolls. What is worse, though, is as members of Congress come and go, many of these unelected bureaucrats stay. Because of their longevity and corresponding corporate knowledge, staff members often become more influential than the elected officials they serve. This unfortunate circumstance means our country is being run less by officials put in office by the people and more by bureaucrats who do not stand for election.

Growth of the Judicial Branch

The growth of the judicial branch of the federal government has nothing to do with the number of judges or how many staff members each judge employs. Rather, the growth of the judicial branch comes from a concept known as *judicial usurpation*. Often referred to as legislating from the bench, judicial usurpation occurs when activist judges ignore the limits prescribed for them in the Constitution and usurp the duties of the Congress.

The growth occurs because of activist judges legislating from the bench, not the size of the court or the number of staff members employed. Judicial usurpation amounts to activist judges making laws instead of ruling on their constitutionality. Every time this unconstitutional act occurs, two things happen—both bad. First, judges gain power they were never intended to have, thereby undermining the checks and balances built into the Constitution by the Founders. Second, American citizens are handed edicts from on high by unelected judges who serve for life and are, therefore, unaccountable to the people. History has proven many times how government officials who are not accountable to the citizens are prone to trample their freedom.

The Founders envisioned judges as neutral, objective interpreters of the Constitution. Alexander Hamilton made this clear. Writing in Federalist 78, Hamilton stated that whereas Congress has the power of the purse and the president the power of the sword, the judiciary has only the power of judgment.[4] Hamilton would be appalled to learn how activist judges—through judicial usurpation—regularly take the power of the purse out of the hands of Congress and the power of the sword out of the hands of the president.

Growth of the National Debt

Federal spending is soaring, and America's national debt is growing by more than a trillion dollars a year. Official projections show rivers of red ink for years to come unless policy makers enact major budget reforms. Unless spending is brought under control, the United States is headed for financial ruin. One of the main reasons for the growth of the national debt is the federal government has expanded into hundreds of areas best left to state and local governments, businesses, charities, and individuals.[5]

Worse yet, Leftist ideologues in Congress have enacted, perpetuated, and expanded so many entitlement programs that half of all Americans derive at least part of their income from the federal government. The ever-increasing level of federal spending is undermining the efficacy of the private sector and creating a government-controlled, socialistic society at odds with traditional American values and what the Founders envisioned for our nation. Cutting federal spending is essential if America is to be saved from the Left.

What You Can Do about Out-of-Control Government

What follows in this section are specific strategies for reducing the size and spending of the federal government. Your role in making these things happen is to support only those political candidates who are willing to make balancing the federal budget and returning the federal government to its constitutional limits part of their political platforms. It is also to monitor sitting members of Congress and hold their feet to the fire concerning this issue. The strategies we recommend are:[6]

- *Department of Agriculture.* End all farm subsidies, cut food subsidies by 50 percent, and end all rural subsidies. These budget cuts will save $87 billion annually and reduce the behemoth Department of Agriculture to a minor government office.

- *Department of Commerce.* End all telecommunication and economic development subsidies. These budget cuts will save $3 billion annually and transform the Department of Commerce into a minor government office.

- *Department of Education.* Eliminate the Department of Education and all its entitlement programs. Much of the funding for such anti-American programs such as Critical Race Theory (CRT) comes from the Department of Education. Taking this step will save $86 billion annually.

- *Department of Energy.* End all subsidies for energy efficiency, vehicle technologies, electricity research, and nuclear energy. These endeavors should be able to stand on their own as private enterprises. Also eliminate the technology loan program and fossil energy research. Privatize the power marketing administrations. These budget cuts would save $21 billion annually and reduce the Department of Energy to a minor government office.

- *Department of Health and Human Services.* Freeze spending on Medicaid, increase Medicare premiums, reduce non-Medicaid state and local grants by 50 percent, increase Medicare deductibles, and enact tort reform. These budget cuts will save $353 billion annually and reduce the Department of Health and Human Services to a minor government office.

- *Department of Housing and Urban Development.* Eliminate the department and all its entitlements. This will save $61 billion annually.

- *Department of Justice.* End all state and local grants. These budget cuts will save $5 billion annually.

- *Department of Labor.* Eliminate all federal employment and training programs, jobs corps, community service for seniors, and trade adjustment assistance. These budget cuts will save $9 billion annually and reduce the Department of Labor to a minor government office.

- *Social Security Administration.* Eliminate price indexing of initial benefits, increase the normal retirement age to seventy, and

reduce the disability program by 10 percent. These minor budget cuts will save $86 billion annually and simultaneously out-
lawing Congress's use of these funds for any other purpose, will
save the social security system from bankruptcy.

- *Department of Transportation.* End all urban transportation
  grants, privatize air traffic control, end all rail subsidies, and
  privatize Amtrak. These budget cuts will save $15 billion annu-
  ally and reduce the Department of Transportation to a minor
  government office.
- *Department of the Treasury.* Cut the earned income tax credit by
  50 percent and eliminate the refundable part of the child tax
  credit. These budget cuts alone will save $46 billion annually.
  Simplifying the tax code to a flat tax for all with reduce the IRS's
  power and scope and allow prosperity to return to our citizens.

Implementing these recommendations would allow the federal government to balance America's budget over a period of ten
years. By making these kinds of cuts—and only by doing so—
can America return to the limited government envisioned by the
Founders and prescribed in the Constitution.

THE ENTITLEMENT MENTALITY REPLACING PERSONAL RESPONSIBILITY

America was largely settled from shore to shore by intrepid individuals who viewed building better lives for themselves and their
families as a do-it-yourself project. They took personal responsibility for their success or failure, asked for nothing more than opportunity, wanted government to stay out of their way, shunned
handouts, and expected to be held accountable for their actions.
Unfortunately, this kind of attitude has changed over time. Overindulgent parents, WOKE school systems, and a nanny government
have resulted in a new attitude toward life best described as an
entitlement mentality.

The entitlement mentality is like a disease affecting the immune
system. It makes people more susceptible to the allure of government bailouts, handouts, and entitlements, and less willing to take
personal responsibility for their lives. Because of decades of Leftist

indoctrination, it has become common for poor people to blame their circumstances on wealthy people, and believe in the redistribution of wealth through taxation and government handouts.

Because of this, American patriots who want to save our country from the Leftist ideologues bent on destroying it must be able to articulate the case for personal responsibility and accountability. The values that made America great will never be restored unless we can overcome the entitlement mentality.

What You Can Do About the Entitlement Mentality

To play a positive role in overcoming the entitlement mentality, patriots must be able to explain convincingly to a new generation of Americans why a willingness to take personal responsibility for their lives—successes and failures—is the best approach in the long run. Being able to articulate the following points about the destructive consequences of the entitlement mentality is important for all American patriots:[7]

- Becoming overly dependent on others or a nanny government makes people dangerously helpless. It breeds a slothful attitude toward life wherein everyone wants to ride in the wagon, and nobody wants to pull it. When this happens, we all suffer, including those riding in the wagon. When everyone is riding in the wagon and no one is pulling, the wagon goes nowhere.
- The entitlement mentality causes people to view the world as inherently unfair and themselves as victims. This is tragic because victims are never victors. Over time people who see themselves as victims respond to the imagined unfairness of life by becoming chronically angry. When this happens, they often act out in counterproductive and even destructive ways (think of the looting, arson, and vandalism that occur so often when peaceful protests morph or are incited into violent riots).
- Entitled people are often fearful of taking the risks essential to success in a competitive society. This fear causes them to seek security from a nanny government which, in turn, makes them even more helpless and dependent on the government.

- For entitled people, failure becomes a self-fulfilling prophecy—
  they expect to fail. Eventually, they come to accept failure as a
  normal way of life instead of an anomaly to be overcome by
  working hard, working smart, and persevering.
- Entitled people often become addicted to counterproductive
  substances. Their rationale can be summarized as follows: "Since
  the world is unfair and the deck is stacked against me, and since
  I can do nothing about it, I will seek solace in drugs and alcohol."
  This unfortunate aspect of the entitlement mentality goes a long
  way toward explaining the opioid and teen suicide crises in
  America today.
- Entitled people struggle to establish and maintain healthy, positive, helpful personal relationships because they are unable to
  trust anyone. Their outlook on life is, "Everybody is out to
  get me."
- Entitled people come to view themselves as permanent victims
  who deserve to be taken care of by other people and a nanny
  government, but the efforts of others and the handouts from
  government are never enough. Not only are they unappreciative
  of the help and handouts, but they are also perpetually angry the
  world does not do more for them.

GREEDY, UNPATRIOTIC CORPORATE EXECUTIVES AND TECHNOLOGY CZARS

Communist leader, Vladimir Ilyich Ulyanov, more commonly
known as Lenin, is reputed to have said, "The capitalists will sell us
the rope with which we will hang them."[8] Whether he said this or
not, the message conveyed is prophetic. For the sake of increasing
profits, there are large corporations in America willing to sell the
United States and its citizens down the river. In fact, quite a few are
doing this right now.

Some large corporations are criticized for maintaining toxic
work environments, providing poor customer service, operating
unethically, and producing shoddy products. But the worst offense
of major corporations is sending American jobs, technologies, and
essential goods (such as pharmaceuticals) overseas to countries har-
boring ill will toward the United States. These countries are

determined to transform America into a backwater nation, and produce products using forced labor, including child labor.

The principal recipient of American jobs and technologies by far is China, a nation bent on America's destruction. India is another major recipient. The obvious attraction of both countries is cheap labor and no regulations. Major corporations that have sent jobs and technologies to China include Morgan Stanley, IBM, Lowe's, GE, Batesville Casket Company, PG&E, Mondelez International, AT&T, Verizon, Microsoft, and QVC to name just a few.

Pharmaceutical companies are among the biggest offenders when it comes to making America dependent on China and India for essential goods. It is now estimated more than 80 percent of the active pharmaceutical ingredients (API) for the prescription drugs used in America come from China and India.[9] The ill-advised nature of sending pharmaceutical manufacturing to China became clear during the COVID-19 pandemic of 2020 and 2021.

It is obvious how Americans are harmed when their jobs are sent overseas, but the even greater harm to our country comes from sending critical technologies to adversarial countries such as China. For an example of this unfortunate phenomenon, consider the case of IBM's relationship with the Chinese company, Teamsun. IBM has licensed critical technologies to Teamsun, a company advised by Shen Changxiang, former supervisor of cybersecurity for China's strategic missile arsenal.

Teamsun has made it clear it plans to "absorb" the technologies, so China no longer needs to depend on American technologies. For the sake of short-term profits, IBM is selling its long-term future. It is no stretch to believe these technologies will eventually become part of the military arsenal aimed by China at the United States. What is IBM's rationale for selling America down the river to our country's number one adversary? What else—sagging profits.[10] This case is a classic example of Lenin's "rope" theory.

Another offense that rankles Americans is technology companies using their monopolies to advance a Leftist agenda while censoring and even denying access to conservatives. The most famous example of this is Twitter and Facebook denying access to President Donald Trump. Social media giants Facebook and Twitter are increasingly under attack from Republicans and Democrats. Calls for eliminating the legal immunity granted to social media platforms in Section 230, using the anti-trust laws to break the companies up, and regulating the platforms are growing louder and more frequent.

What You Can Do about Greedy Corporate Executives Technology Czars

When criticized for sending American jobs to China, greedy corporate executives often claim doing so makes them more competitive, and competition is a good thing. Competition is a good thing if it is fair and occurs on a level playing field. However, this is not what happens when jobs are sent to China. The Chinese government subsidizes its businesses to give them an edge over American companies, and it uses forced labor—including child labor—to perform jobs American workers are paid to do. Further, China "absorbs"—read steals and reverse engineers—technologies from American firms and uses them to undermine our superiority in business and national defense.

Jason Miller responded to President Trump being canceled by Twitter by founding his own social media platform: GETTR. The goal of GETTR, according to Jason Miller, is "fighting cancel culture, promoting common sense, defending free speech, challenging social media monopolies, and creating a true marketplace of ideas."[11] This is an excellent way to fight back against the political and cultural bias of the established social media giants, but it is not an option most Americans have.

Donald Trump has since launched TruthSocial to huge initial success, lead by former congressman Devin Nunes. Donald Trump has the resources to establish his own social media platform; most Americans do not. However, there is much you can do about greedy corporate executives and technology czars.

- Support only those politicians who are willing to level the playing field when it comes to competing with China through tariffs, tax cuts for businesses manufacturing products in the United States, and other means.

- Demand politicians bar American companies from sharing critical technologies with Chinese companies and apply stiff penalties for those that do.
- Demand transparent, unannounced inspections of Chinese facilities to ensure forced labor and child labor are not used in the manufacture of products.
- Invest in and/or join alternative social media platforms and stop using Facebook and Twitter.
- Demand elected officials remove the Section 230 protections from social media platforms that discriminate based on politics, break up the social media giants, or both.

RISING TIDE OF ANARCHY

Anarchy is the rejection of societal laws and the governing bodies enforcing them. Said another way, anarchy is mob rule. We face a rising tide of anarchy in America as criminals and other bad actors foment tribal discord based on perceived and, often, manufactured societal inequities. Paid out-of-state instigators have become particularly adept at transforming peaceful protests into violent riots characterized by looting, vandalism, arson, and bullying. These same criminal instigators were behind the defund-the-police movement in 2020 that received support from numerous Leftist mayors, city council members, and federal politicians.

According to the Major Cities Chiefs Association (MCCA), in 2020 there were 574 violent riots in America's larger cities. Some of the participants in these riots were motivated by "extreme anti-government or anti-law enforcement ideologies. . . . Others simply used the protests as cover to engage in criminal behavior." During the 2020 riots, ninety-seven police cars were burned, 2,037 police officers were injured, and several police precincts were set on fire.[12] Rioters did not limit themselves to weapons such as rocks, bricks, baseball bats, and frozen water bottles. Firearms and incendiary devices such as Molotov cocktails were used in half of the riots.[13]

Although Leftist ideologues and weak-kneed public officials tried to claim the riots were justifiable protests by local citizens over perceived injustices, MCCA found 90 percent of the police agencies involved discovered out-of-state individuals participating in the riots. Worse yet, 29 percent of the police agencies involved discovered individuals being paid to participate in the riots.[14] MCCA identified the following tactics widely used by outside instigators, paid participants, and local protestors who joined forces with the instigators:[15]

- Staging in advance of riots
- Bringing in out-of-town participants
- Concealing weapons in "snack vans"
- Listening in on police broadcasts
- Using bicycle scouts to provide information on police locations and activities
- Using barricades against the police
- Freeing arrested rioters from police custody.

One of the most disturbing aspects of the riots in America's larger cities was the lack of support law-enforcement agencies received from elected officials. The Leftist ideologues who control many of America's larger cities sided with the rioters who were burning their cities down instead of the police officers who were trying to restore order and protect the citizens. According to the MCCA, 46 percent of the police departments responding to the riots reported "experiencing low or very low support from elected officials."[16]

What You Can Do about the Rising Tide of Anarchy

Defunding the police and siding with rioters bent on burning down and looting large cities was foolishness in the extreme, something even Leftist elected officials are learning. Major cities that defunded their police departments include New York, Washington, DC, Baltimore, Philadelphia, Los Angeles, San Francisco, Atlanta, Minneapolis, Seattle, Salt Lake City, Portland (Oregon), Hartford (Connecticut), Norman (Oklahoma), and Austin (Texas).

Predictably, all these cities experienced rapid increases in violent crime. For example, in Minneapolis, homicides increased by 60 percent. Atlanta experienced its most violent year on record. According to the National Police Support Fund, "Sadly, this scenario continues to play out in cities across the country that continue the push to defund the police. Expect even more homicides and violent crimes this year as budgetary changes passed in 2020 go into effect in 2021."[17]

To do your part on reversing the rising tide of anarchy, arm yourself with the information in this section and use it when you interact with elected officials in your community. Refuse to support an elected official or political candidate at any level who does not openly and proudly support law and order and the police officers who maintain it. Demand sitting elected officials who support defunding the police be held accountable for the resulting violent crime.

WOKE MILITARY LEADERSHIP AND AN UNPEPARED MILITARY

The most dangerous of the internal threats to America's end game is the social justice agenda of top-ranking military leaders. WOKE-NESS has infiltrated our military at the highest levels and cascaded down through the ranks to the point political correctness has become more important to a successful career than military competence. This unfortunate shift in priorities calls into question our military's ability to conduct its mission of defending the United States against all enemies foreign and domestic.

Victor Davis Hanson, Senior Fellow at the Hoover Institution, prophetically claims the Pentagon's current agenda ". . . has resulted in too many various emphases on domestic cultural, social, and political issues. And naturally, as a result, there is less attention given to winning wars and leveraging such victories to our nation's strategic advantage."[18] Said another way, while communist China is focused on developing hypersonic missiles for which the U.S. has no answer, our military is focused on providing sex-change operations for transgendered troops and forcing personnel at all levels to

undergo training in Critical Race Theory. The potential consequences of the military's loss of mission focus ". . . are downright
scary for a world superpower upon which millions at home and
billions worldwide depend."[19]

The culture of WOKENESS influences who joins the various
services and who rises through the ranks. More and more, people
who join the military for the traditional reasons are being weeded
out by a politically correct system or are leaving of their own accord
out of disgust for the system. Military politicians are replacing warriors. In the meantime, such traditional essentials as physical fitness,
proficiency with weapons, and small unit tactics are suffering.

In 2021, WOKE military leaders began using the COVID-19
vaccination mandate to weed out officers and enlisted troops who
refuse to toe the line of Leftist orthodoxy. The mandate "Is being
used as a vehicle to target those conservative minded individuals
that have strong religious opinions, or are free thinkers, or just
don't see the need . . . but hold more conservative values. This is
just an opportunity to use regulation and the vehicle of the shot
to weed these people out because those same people are the nay-
sayers or those that are providing pushback to the 'wokeism' invad-
ing the military."[20]

What You Can Do about WOKENESS and Unpreparedness in the Military

Leftist ideologues in Congress are experts at praising the military
in public and undermining it in private. Worse yet, some high-
ranking military leaders are experts at determining which way the
political winds are blowing and then, going in the same direction.
Their highest goal is protecting their careers and building up their
pensions, not defending the United States against all enemies foreign and domestic.

In the process, they become sycophantic lap dogs for politicians whose support they need to further their careers. Therefore,
so many high-ranking officers have become advocates of Leftist
orthodoxy, and why they are forcing this destructive ideology on
our troops at all levels. WOKENESS is leading to unpreparedness
in the military. To help reverse this course, you must understand

and be able to articulate the need for maintaining the best-trained, best-equipped, and best-led military in the world. Here are several key points you must be able to articulate when talking with elected officials, candidates for high office, and WOKE advocates you meet:

- America is at war right now. We are engaged in a deadly cold war with China and an ongoing war with international terrorist groups. We could be engaged in a hot war at any moment with North Korea or Iran. China, North Korea, Iran, and international terrorist organizations have no interest in peace, nor are they interested in negotiating except as a tactic for stalling while they plan the downfall of the United States. These nations and organizations are interested only in dominance and know they must destroy the United States or weaken us to the point of irrelevance to achieve that goal. These bad actors do not think like we think, do not share our values, nor do they respond to reason. They respect only two things: strength and the resolve to use it. Consequently, any perceived lack of strength or resolve on America's part invites aggression on their part.

- There has never been a time in the history of our country when having a strong, well-quipped, properly trained, and fully supported military was more important. This means all attempts to finance the social programs of Leftist ideologues by pulling funding away from the military must be rejected outright. The world is a dangerous place for freedom-loving people. There is only one way to prevent wars in the current global environment: field the best-trained, best-equipped, best-led, and best-funded military in the world—a military that can quickly and effectively make the cost of attacking the United States too high to even contemplate.

- Understand our enemies know and appreciate what is happening in our military. They know about the culture of WOKENESS and what it is doing to military preparedness. According to Victor Davis Hanson, "Our enemies hope that the once most powerful military in the history of civilization is going through a sort of people's liberation army revolution, one in which ideological purity, not battlefield competence, is deemed the better measure of today's high-ranking officer corps."[21]

ILLEGAL IMMIGRATION AT THE SOUTHERN BORDER

As president, Donald Trump took strong and decisive steps to gain control of America's southern border. When Joe Biden became president, he immediately undid all the Trump administration's good work and hung out a *welcome sign* inviting immigrants to enter our country illegally. Not surprisingly, illegal immigrants responded in numbers unprecedented in America's history. Within just weeks of taking office, President Biden and his Leftist puppet masters lost control of the border creating an immigration, health, and humanitarian disaster.

During President Biden's first year in office two million immigrants from 160 countries—147,000 of them unaccompanied children—tried to enter the United States illegally.[22] The southern border has become a cesspool of crime and corruption. Drug dealers, sex traffickers, and "coyotes" who charge immigrants thousands of dollars to sneak them across the border prey on the unaccompanied immigrant children and women. While the United States was enduring a COVID-19 pandemic, thousands of infected immigrants were allowed to cross the border and stay.

"New and more dangerous variants of the COVID virus threaten to send the nation back into some form of lockdown. But even as hospital wards are filling, and new restrictions on personal freedoms are being imposed, migrants carrying the virus and its vaccine-resistant variants are being released into the United States and settled in communities across the country."[23] More than 40,000 COVID-infected illegal immigrants were released into the United States by the Biden administration in 2021.[24]

The disaster at America's southern border has been a windfall for international drug cartels. The cartels are funding illegal immigration into the United States and using illegal immigrants desperate to gain entry as drug mules and drug dealers for the cartels. "There is now evidence that the Chinese Communist Party is working hand in hand with the Cartels on illegal drug (particularly Fentanyl) shipments into the heart of America."[25]

What You Can Do about Illegal Immigration

To play a positive role in solving the crisis at America's southern border, make illegal immigration an issue when you talk with your representatives in Congress and when choosing which political candidates to support for election or re-election. The Stand Up America US Foundation recommends treating the cartels like what they are: terrorist groups. Support only those candidates who are willing to instruct police and the military to go on the offensive against the international drug cartels. They are making war on America—we should make war on them. Undertake special operations missions against the cartels and put them out of business.[26]

In addition to going on the offensive against the drug cartels, there are other specific actions you can support. The following recommendations came out of a meeting of twenty-five U.S. governors who met in McAllen, Texas, for the purpose of drafting recommendations they, in turn, sent to President Biden:[27]

- Continue Title 42 public health restrictions so COVID-19 infected individuals trying to cross the border can be denied entrance.
- Fully reinstate the Migrant Protection Protocols (MPP) requiring asylum seekers to return to Mexico until their court hearing.
- Complete the wall begun during the Trump administration.
- End "catch and release" so apprehended illegal immigrants are no longer released into the United States.
- Clear the judicial backlog. Dedicate additional judges and resources to U.S. immigration courts.
- Resume deportation of all criminals caught crossing the border. Enforce all deportation laws pertaining to convicted illegal immigrants.
- Dedicate the resources necessary to eliminate human trafficking and drug trafficking.

- Reestablish the agreements from the previous administration with the Northern Triangle countries (El Salvador, Guatemala, and Honduras) and Mexico to control their own borders.
- Send a clear message to illegal immigrants that the door to America is now closed to all except those who seek entry through legal channels.
- Deploy more federal law-enforcement officers to the border.

Overcoming the domestic threats to America's end game for the twenty-first century will not be easy. It will require a concerted effort on the part of all patriots who want to save our country from the Leftist ideologues who are trying to destroy it. It might even require the work of more than one generation, but it can be done. The strategies set forth in this chapter will help you play a positive role in winning the battle for America's soul.

COMPROMISED ELECTION SYSTEM

One of the biggest threats, not just to America's end game for the twenty-first century but to our republican form of government, is our compromised election system. Unless we take the steps necessary to make sure elections at all levels are fair, impartial, and transparent, the Marxist ideologues who are determined to destroy America will win without a fight. This is not just speculation or hyperbole on our parts. As became evident in the aftermath of the Trump-Biden presidential election, election fraud is a harsh reality that must be faced and overcome.

Although Democrats go to great lengths to deny voter fraud occurred in the Trump/Biden election, legitimate questions were raised for which satisfactory answers have yet to be provided. Here are just a few of the questions about voter fraud that have gone unanswered and must be answered before the 2022 mid-term elections and the 2024 presidential election:

- What role did computer hacking by the Chinese Communist Party (CCP) and Pakistan ISI play in the election results, particularly in the key battleground states of Arizona, Nevada, Wisconsin, Michigan, Pennsylvania, and Georgia?

- Were voting machines provided by Dominion Voting Systems Corporation secure or could they be tampered with?
- Were the signatures on absentee ballots properly checked?
- Why were there so many affidavits from witnesses claiming knowledge of voter fraud attached to lawsuits filed challenging the election results?
- Why were counties allowed to mail out ballots en masse even when they had not been requested?
- Why were counties allowed to violate their own state laws concerning the counting of mail-in ballots?

These are all legitimate questions that must be answered satisfactorily before the 2022 mid-term elections and the 2024 presidential election. Your job as an American patriot is to demand your state legislature take the necessary steps to prevent voter fraud of any kind in upcoming elections at all levels.

CHAPTER 8

OVERCOMING FOREIGN THREATS TO THE END GAME

To accomplish the various steps in the blueprint for saving America, it will be necessary to overcome several specific domestic and foreign threats standing in the way. This chapter explains how to overcome the foreign threats that could derail the blueprint for saving America.

FOREIGN THREATS TO THE END GAME THAT MUST BE OVERCOME

To save America from the Leftist ideologues who want to destroy our country, patriots must join and overcome the following foreign threats:

- Cold War and Communist China's plans for world dominance
- Russia's threat to America's vital national interests
- Iran's nuclear program and support of terrorists
- International drug cartels
- New caliphate in Afghanistan
- Unconventional warfare: cyber, biological, viral, and space
- International shadow government/"fifth column"

COLD WAR AND COMMUNIST CHINA'S PLANS FOR WORLD DOMINANCE

In September 2021, President Joe Biden announced to the 76th session of the United Nation's General Assembly (UNGA) the United States did not seek a cold war with China. This was a stunning proclamation since America is already in a cold war with China and we are losing the war. The president's comment must have pleased the UN delegation of the People's Republic of China's (PRC). After all, Sun Tzu—the legendary Chinese military strategist—wrote it is easier to win a war when your opponent does not realize he is already at war.

The PRC has made clear its ambition for global domination, and it is pursuing this end far more effectively than did Soviet leaders during the first Cold War. Xi Jinping, Communist China's "President for life," aims to avoid Soviet mistakes and has developed a comprehensive plan for winning the new cold war.

The first objective of Xi Jinping's plan is to achieve overwhelming military strength—a goal now within reach. Their annual military budget has increased every year for more than two decades. The PRC now has the largest military on earth based on manpower, numbers of ships, tanks, aircraft, and advanced technologies, including space warfare capabilities.

The second element of the PRC plan is to buy influence around the globe. The Soviets, lacking China's financial wherewithal, used military threats and KGB extortion to coerce second and third world leaders to become satellite Soviet Republics. The PRC will use threats and coercion only when all else fails.

The third part of the PRC strategy is to use cheap labor, foreign investment capital, stolen intellectual property, and trade violations to make Communist China the world's most powerful economy. Xi Jinping knows economic failures brought down the Soviet Union in the 1980s.

The PRC will of course continue conducting propaganda, espionage, and illegal trade activities against the U.S. and Europe. But elsewhere, in Africa, Southwest Asia, Oceania, and the Middle East—it is all about acquiring minerals, rare earth minerals, even hydrocarbon fuel—and real estate in strategic locations. China has already made its move to secure relations with the Taliban in Afghanistan to gain access to that country's mineral wealth and to gain control of Bagram Air Base, the best military facility in Southwest Asia.

The strategies the PRC is using to win the cold war with the United States are explained in this chapter along with what can be done to overcome its leading position and win the second cold war just as America won the first Cold War. The People's Republic of China (PRC)—communist China—is aggressively pursuing a long-range strategic plan for world dominance by the year 2049. This date is significant to the Chinese Communist Party (CCP) because it marks the 100th anniversary of the establishment of the PRC as declared by the leader of the CCP, Mao Zedong, on October 1, 1949. Unless patriots come together to achieve America's end game, accomplishing world dominance will not take the PRC that long.

Here is what the U.S. State Department had to say about the PRC's plan for world dominance during the Trump administration:

> Awareness has been growing in the United States—and in nations around the world—that the Chinese Communist Party (CCP) has triggered a new era of great power competition. Yet few discern the pattern in China's inroads within every region of the world, much less the specific form of dominance to which the party aspires. The CCP aims not merely at preeminence within the established world order— and order that is grounded in free and sovereign nation-states, flows from the universal principles on which America was founded, and advances U.S. national interests—but to fundamentally revise world order, placing the People's Republic of China (PRC) at the center and serving Beijing's authoritarian goals and hegemonic ambitions.[1]

The three highest priority elements of the PRC's strategic plan for achieving world dominance are: 1) complete control of the Chinese people—and the people of any other nations falling under its dominance—through authoritarian governance, 2) using economic incentives and coercion to out influence the United States in every region of the world and in international organizations, and 3) developing a world-class military surpassing that of the United States.[2]

In keeping with its Marxist-Leninist roots, the CCP enforces strict authoritarian rule over the Chinese people. Control is maintained through the "... systematic use of indoctrination, censorship, disinformation, high-tech surveillance, forced disappearances, and other brutal means."[3] Dissent is quickly and violently suppressed as was seen during the pro-democracy protests in Tiananmen Square in 1989. Students conducting a peaceful protest were attacked and overrun by the PRC's military which deployed tanks against the unarmed students killing and wounding thousands. The CCP will enforce the same authoritarian rule over any country that comes under its dominance.

The second high priority element in the PRC's strategic plan for world dominance is "economic co-optation and coercion."[4] This element amounts to using access to Chinese markets and its low-cost labor force to make other nations economically dependent on the PRC, then leveraging that dependence to gain influence. The United States has already fallen into this trap. Seeking low-cost labor, America has exported almost three million jobs to China. Seeking low-cost goods, the United States receives 19 percent of its imported goods from the PRC. These goods used to be limited to cheap consumer products but now include expensive essentials such as medical equipment, pharmaceuticals, and advanced electronics.

Tactics included in the economic element of the PRC's strategic plan for world dominance include massive, aggressive theft of intellectual property and technologies from advanced nations such as the United States, control over supply chains for essential goods (e.g., pharmaceuticals and medical equipment), industrial dominance through manufacturing superiority, building the world's fifth generation wireless telecommunication infrastructure to gain dominance in emerging information technologies, making poorer countries dependent on China for critical infrastructure projects (e.g., airports, railroads, highways, dams, bridges, etc.), unregulated access to foreign capital markets such as the American stock exchanges, and exploitation of the openness of the world's democratic nations to steal technology, trade secrets, proprietary data, and the results of research and development.[5]

The third high-priority element in the PRC's strategic plan for world hegemony is building the largest, best-equipped, most capable military in the world. The specific goal of this element of the plan is to surpass the United States military on land, in the air, on the water, under the water, and in space. Tactics included in this element of the plan include:[6]

- "Military-Civil Fusion." This tactic amounts to acquiring through any means—including illegal means—the most advanced technologies from countries around the world and adapting them for military uses.
- "Systems-destruction warfare." This tactic amounts to attacking and shutting down command and control centers and operational systems. Its emphasis is cyber warfare.
- Amassing vast arsenals of ground-based precision missiles to penetrate American defenses. This tactic includes development of hypersonic (Mach 5) missiles such as the one the PRC is believed to have evaluated in October 2021. This missile is a nuclear-capable hypersonic glide vehicle that flew through low-orbit space, circling the globe before striking close to its target. Bear in mind, with nuclear weapons "near the target" is near enough. Hypersonic missiles of this type are a direct threat to the United States.
- "Assassin's Mace." This tactic amounts to surprising adversaries from unexpected vectors.
- Industrial dominance. This tactic amounts to gaining the type of manufacturing dominance that was such a factor in helping the United States play a major role in winning World War II and becoming the arsenal of democracy. This tactic includes gaining world leadership in artificial intelligence.
- Space warfare. The PRC is aggressively developing its space warfare capabilities. It already can target and shoot down U.S. satellites. The PRC's space force is a component of the Peoples' Liberation Army (PLA). It is focused on developing and

deploying maneuverable re-entry vehicles, hypersonic weapons, directed-energy weapons, electromagnetic railguns, counter-space weapons, unmanned vehicles, and artificial intelligence weapons. Space warfare threats are covered in more depth later in this chapter.

- Biological and viral weapons. Although the PRC is intensely secretive about its biological and viral weapons capabilities, it is believed to have an advanced program including research, development, production, and weaponization capabilities. The COVID-19 pandemic's worldwide spread in 2020 after the virus was released from a laboratory in Wuhan, China, is an example of the PRC's capabilities. Biological and viral warfare threats are covered in more depth later in this chapter.

- The PRC's "Belt and Road Initiative." President Xi Jinping introduced the PRC's "Belt and Road" strategy in 2013. The purpose of this strategy is to "buy" influence in countries across the globe by financing major infrastructure projects in those countries. To date, the PRC has invested an estimated $100 billion in his kind of project in Iran, Venezuela, South Africa, Kenya, Tanzania, Indonesia, and Brazil. The unstated purpose of the Belt and Road strategy is to make recipient countries debtors to the PRC. Once these countries are deeply in debt to the PRC, the Chinese Communist Party (CCP) can use the debt to gain control over them. The PRC has also taken advantage of the economic difficulties countries around the world have suffered from the COVID-19 pandemic by offering loans to these countries. Once again, the goal is to gain control of them by making these countries debtors to the PRC. The debtor nations become PRC allies—coerced puppet states are a better description—because they have no choice.

- The PRC's designs on Afghanistan. The United States had not even completed its poorly-planned, disastrous evacuation of Afghanistan before the PRC began moving in to buy influence with the cash-strapped Taliban. The PRC covets the mineral resources of Afghanistan and Bagram Air Base, the most advanced military base in Southwest Asia. Because of the incompetent handling of America's exit from Afghanistan, the PRC has an open door to gaining influence if not control over that country. The PRC plans to use Bagram Airbase as its forward outpost in Southwest Asia. PRC aircraft have already been spotted at Bagram. Having the use of Bagram Airbase gives the PRC maximum access to Afghanistan for getting personnel in and out, for bringing out valuable mineral resources, and for use in military operations.

- The PRC's nuclear arsenal. The PRC is expected to have at least one-thousand nuclear warheads by 2030 and is in the process of building missile silos for nuclear-tipped intercontinental ballistic missiles.

The PRC is not just planning, it is putting massive amounts of funding behind its plans. Although the United States still spends the most on its military, the PRC is working hard and fast to catch up. Since 1992 the PRC has increased its military spending by 800 percent, a percentage dwarfing corresponding increases by the United States.

What is even worse is how the American military is spending its money. The United States is spending large portions of its military budget on non-military expenditures such as across-the-board training in Critical Race Theory (CRT) and other social justice concepts. While Americans troops are being forced to complete CRT training, the PRC is developing nuclear-capable hypersonic missiles for which the U.S. military currently has no defense.

What You Can Do about China's Plans for World Dominance

Taking on the PRC might seem like an impossible task for American patriots, but it is not. Our job as patriots who want to save America is to know what needs to be done by the powerbrokers in Washington, DC and the Pentagon, and demand they do what is necessary. This section contains a list of things the United States must do to prevent world dominance by the PRC. Memorize these strategies and share them with your representatives in Congress.

Support only those elected officials and political candidates who are willing to commit to achieving the following:[7]

- Secure freedom at home by preserving the Constitution and Bill of Rights, fostering economic prosperity, and strengthening the bonds of American society.
- Maintain the most powerful, best-equipped, best-led, best-trained, and most agile military in the world on land, in the air, on the sea, and in space while fostering cooperation among with and among our allies.
- Bolster the international order established following World War II which is composed of sovereign nations that respect human rights and fidelity to the rule of law.
- Promote American interests when dealing with the PRC while, at the same time, seeking opportunities to cooperate based on the norms of reciprocity and fairness. In seeking such opportunities, the United States must be prepared to deter the PRC when circumstances require it.
- Educate the American public about the implications of the challenges America faces from the PRC's plans for world dominance so citizens support the policies and actions required to secure freedom.
- Train a new generation of public servants and public policy makers who will be fluent in Chinese, knowledgeable of Chinese culture and history, and able to use their knowledge to protect and advance America's diplomatic, military, economic, scientific, and technological interests.
- Reform American education so students understand America's legacy of freedom and liberty and are, as a result, equipped to take on the responsibilities of citizenship in a free constitutional republic society.
- Demonstrate to the world how freedom, liberty, and the other cornerstone principles upon which our country was founded are superior to authoritarian control, indoctrination, and blind obedience characterizing the PRC's system through public diplomacy, educational initiatives, foreign assistance and investment, and sanctions when necessary.

The Office of the Secretary of State during the administration of President Donald Trump summarized America's challenge in these words:

> Grounded in America's founding principles and constitutional traditions; invigorated by a bustling economy; undergirded by the world's best-trained and best-equipped military; served by government officials who understand the American people and the American political system, recognize the diversity and common humanity of the peoples and nations of the world, and appreciate the complex interplay of ideas and interests in foreign affairs; and fortified by an informed and engaged citizenry—this multi-pronged approach will enable the United States to secure freedom.[8]

RUSSIA'S THREAT TO AMERICA'S VITAL NATIONAL INTERESTS

Many Americans are under the impression Russia is no longer a threat to America's vital interests. They think the fall of the former Soviet Union left Russia weakened and irrelevant. This is a badly mistaken impression. In some ways, the threat is greater now than during the Soviet era because the Russia of today is like a wounded wolf. Under Vladimir Putin, Russia is determined to regain its former place on the world stage, and it views the United States and its NATO allies as major stumbling blocks to its ambitions.

Alexis Mrachek of the Heritage Foundation sounded the alarm when she summarized the Russian threat in October of 2021 in these words:

> Russia remains a formidable threat to the United States and its interests in Europe. From the Arctic to the Baltics, Ukraine, and the South Caucasus, and increasingly in the Mediterranean, Russia continues to foment instability in Europe. Russia remains antagonistic to the United States both militarily and politically. . . . Russia uses its energy position, along with espionage, cyberattacks, and information warfare, to exploit vulnerabilities with the goal of dividing

the transatlantic alliance and undermining faith in government and societal institutions.[9]

These strategies represent major challenges for the United States and its allies, but the most formidable threat from Russia remains its potential for military aggression. The Russian military is still strong and, under the direction of Vladimir Putin, is being modernized and strengthened significantly. In 2020, Russia invested $62 billion in its military and remained one of the top five nations in the world in defense spending.[10]

"Russia is the only state adversary in the Europe region that possesses the capability to threaten the U.S. homeland with conventional and nonconventional means. Although there is no indication that Russia plans to use its capabilities against the United States absent a broader conflict involving America's NATO allies, the plausible potential for such a scenario serves to sustain the strategic importance of those capabilities."[11] Add to Russia's military strength its cyberattack capabilities—it has already interfered with a presidential election in the United States. They have a history of espionage, talent for salacious propaganda, and its long-standing antipathy toward the United States, and it is easy to see why that country remains a significant threat to America's vital national interests.

This all came to life-shattering reality when Russia invaded Ukraine on February 24, 2022. Putin's avarice and brutality chased millions of Ukrainians from their homes and even out of the country as he targeted civilian women and children. At this writing, the valiant patriots of Ukraine led by their unflinching president, Volodymyr Zelenskyy, are putting up a fight the Russian dictator did not expect.

From early on in his invasion, Putin threated nuclear war against any country that interfered and as his troops faltered in March, he added threats of cyberattacks. To the detriment of Ukraine, U.S. security, and the world at large, President Biden and his hapless VP have taken every opportunity to show confusion and ineptitude. There's a substantial argument to be made that Biden purposefully avoided doing what could have prevented Putin's aggression before it started taking innocent lives.

What You Can Do about Russia's Threat to America's Vital National Interests

As with the threats from the People's Republic of China (PRC), taking on Russia must seem like a formidable if not impossible challenge. While the challenge is formidable, it is possible. As it is with the China threat, our job as patriots who want to save America is to know what the powerbrokers in Washington, DC and the Pentagon must do to counter the Russian threat and demand they do what is necessary.

This section contains things the United States must do to counter the Russian threat. Memorize these strategies and share them with your representatives in Congress. Support only those elected officials and political candidates who will commit to achieving the following strategies:

- Maintain the most powerful, best-equipped, best-trained, and best-led military in the world on land, in the air, on the sea, and in space.
- Maintain close mutually-beneficial relationships with our NATO allies and demand they do their part in deterring Russian aggression.
- Develop effective countermeasures to prevent cyberattacks and to respond in kind to them.
- Redouble our efforts to take out Russian espionage rings in the United States and Europe.
- Counter Russian propaganda aimed at driving a wedge between the United States and its NATO allies with our own positive, truthful information dissemination programs.
- Perhaps most importantly, we must take steps to once again become an energy-independent country America was during the presidency of Donald Trump so Russia cannot use its energy resources for leverage on the world stage as Putin did leading up to his war on Ukraine.

Russia remains a threat to America's vital national interests as well as those of our NATO allies. However, if our country takes the steps recommended herein, America can negate the threats from Russia and ensure our freedom and liberty for decades to come. As a patriot, your role is to demand elected officials and decision makers in the Pentagon take these necessary steps.

Russia also wants more positive engagement from the U.S. During Trump's tenure, Russia was constantly being maligned and bombarded by the U.S. press/media and the Congress. I (General Vallely) met with Ambassador Michael Bogdonov, Putin's top deputy for the Middle East on several occasions. In Paris and Moscow, we set up the first meeting between Trump and Putin at the G20 meeting in June 2017. The Russians wanted to follow through on engagements with the U.S. and Trump, but the Russian collusion hoax and follow-up "kangaroo" impeachment hearings negated all positive initiatives.

IRAN'S NUCLEAR PROGRAM AND SUPPORT OF TERRORISTS

"For decades, the United States and the international community have mobilized to prevent a nuclear-armed Iran, believing that nuclear weapons in the hands of the Iranian regime would directly threaten Israel, destabilize the region, and present a security risk to the U.S., Europe, and other allies."[12] Because a nuclear-armed Iran threatens Israel, Europe, and other American allies such as Saudi Arabia, Bahrain, and the UAE, it has the potential to start a nuclear conflagration the United States would soon and inevitably be pulled into.

Nuclear capability would encourage increased aggressiveness on the part of an already aggressive Iran. Its use of terrorist proxies such as Hezbollah and Hamas for attacking Israel would increase as it held the Middle East and Israel's allies, including the United States, hostage by threatening to go nuclear in its attacks. Iran already has the ability to hit the United States with conventional weapons. Arming this rogue nation with nuclear weapons would increase the threat it already represents to the free world exponentially.

In addition to the nuclear threat, Iran is the world's leading state sponsor of terrorism. This rogue nation has been designated a state sponsor of terrorism since 1984. It finances and equips such terrorist organizations as Hezbollah, Hamas, Al-Qaeda, the Islamic Revolutionary Guard Corps-Quds Force, and Iraqi Shia terrorist groups including Kataib Hezbollah, Harakat al Nujaba, and Asaib al-Haq. In addition to financing and equipping terrorist groups, Iran maintains a highly capable cyberattack program it uses against foreign governments and private sector businesses.[13]

What You Can Do about Iran's Nuclear Program and Sponsorship of Terrorism

Leftists in the Biden administration and Democrat Party are determined to resurrect a nuclear deal with Iran. To review, in 2015 several countries—including the United States—signed a nuclear agreement with Iran known as the Joint Comprehensive Plan of Action (JCPOA). In signing the JCPOA, Iran agreed to shut down much of its nuclear program and allow inspections for verification. Not surprisingly, Iran failed to live up to the agreement. As a result, in 2018 President Donald Trump pulled the United States out of the JCPOA.

As result of Trump's actions, Iran resumed its nuclear program or, at least, this is what its leaders claim. The truth is, Iran never stopped developing nuclear material despite the deal, which is why Trump pulled the United States out of JCPOA and imposed strict economic sanctions on Iran. True to form, Iran used the nuclear deal to gain time while lulling the United States and other signatory nations into complacency.

Iran is a rogue nation bent on the destruction of Israel and the United States and has no intention of ever keeping its word on any treaty. For this reason, it is important for patriots to understand a treaty with Iran on nuclear weapons will not prevent Iran from becoming a nuclear armed country despite the wishful thinking of weak-kneed leaders in the West, including the United States. With this point made, here is what you can do about Iran's nuclear program:

- Understand and be able to articular to elected officials and political candidates why resurrecting JCPOA in any form is a bad idea. Here are several reasons why this is true: 1) Iran will not comply with any nuclear deal and will find ways to cheat on its provisions, 2) A deal will not stop Iran from becoming a nuclear state in the future (a deal is just an ill-advised attempt at finding a short-term solution to a long-term problem), 3) Iran cheated on the original nuclear deal by continuing to test missiles so why would any sane person expect them to comply with a new deal?, and 4) A nuclear deal Iran will not comply with leaves Israel vulnerable to a future nuclear attack. 5) The deal would actually help finance Iran's lust for nuclear weapons and the ability to deliver them anywhere in the world.

- Accept the hard truth that neither a nuclear deal with Iran nor even the toughest economic sanctions will stop that rogue nation from becoming a nuclear state. The only viable and permanent solution to the nuclear threat from Iran is the military option. Israel has stated openly and with unwavering commitment it will not allow Iran to become a nuclear state and has shown through its past actions against Iraq and Syria it means business. The job of the United States, then, is to support Israel when the time comes for military action. International pressure on Israel against taking military action will be intense. The United States will have to stand strong with Israel. The job of American patriots is to send a loud and clear message to Washington, DC, demanding the United States stand with Israel in disarming Iran.

- As to Iran's support of terrorism and defeating terrorism in general, we also recommend a more robust military response. If we are in a war on terrorism, then we should make war on terrorists and give up on nation building and outdated counterinsurgency (COIN) methods that grew out of World War II. The course of action we recommend is called "The Lily Pad Strategy."[14] Developed by one of the authors, Major General (Ret.) Paul Vallely, the Lily Pad Strategy and Joint Strike Force Operations is an innovative warfighting strategy for military operations designed to replace traditional Counterinsurgency (COIN) doctrine and nation building. As was shown by our twenty-year war in Afghanistan, traditional COIN doctrine and nation building do not work. Following America's barely

planned, ineptly executed, catastrophic exit from Afghanistan—
an effort fumbled badly by the administration of President Joe
Biden—the Taliban, once again, control the country and international terrorist groups are eyeing Afghanistan as a haven for
conducting their nefarious operations, particularly against the
United States. So much for COIN doctrine and nation building.
Vallely describes the Lily Pad Strategy as follows: ". . . forward
overt and covert bases (lily pads) from which U.S. and other
forces could plan and execute operational missions to lay siege
to the centers of gravity of all enemy jihadi activity and secure
the areas and convert them to safe zones. From the 'lily pad'
locations, coordination of regional states/forces will be accomplished to fight and destroy ISIS (or other terrorist groups),
international threats such as Cartels and other identifiable
threats to America and its citizens. The 'lily pad' forward bases
are of three types: 1) Type A existing geographical bases already
owned, or used by U.S. forces, 2) Type B international bases
controlled/owned by foreign friendly countries providing access
to U.S. and other friendly forces, and 3) Type 3 covert bases.
An eight to twelve ship aircraft carrier group would be considered a 'lily pad.'"[15] Your job as an American patriot in helping
defeat America's enemies is to support strategies such as the Lily
Pad Strategy and make your representatives in the House and
Senate aware of this strategy. If the twenty-year war in Afghanistan proved anything, it proved outmoded doctrines such
COIN and nation building will not defeat terrorism. The Lily
Pad Strategy emphasizes swift responses to neutralize all targets.
It does not require the stationing of large numbers of troops and
equipment overseas, instead relying on a strike-quickly-and-
return-home methodology. It also makes maximum use of over
the horizon technologies such as missiles and space weapons,
cyber warfare, and psychological operations.

INTERNATIONAL DRUG CARTELS

According to the United States Department of Justice, "Drug cartels
are large, sophisticated organizations composed of multiple DTOs

(drug trafficking organizations) and cells with specific assignments such as drug transportation, security/enforcement, or money laundering. Drug cartel command-and-control structures are based outside the United States; however, they produce, transport, and distribute illicit drugs domestically with the assistance of DTOs that are either part of or in alliance with the cartel."[16]

Drugs have become a scourge on American society. For example, narco-slaves on American farms have become a major problem. It is estimated 10,000 migrant workers have been forced to work on illegal growing operations—enterprises generating more than a billion dollars annually. The cartels use hemp farm operations as cover for growing marijuana. There are 70,000 deaths per year from drug overdoses in the United States. Twenty percent of federal and state prisoners committed the crimes that led to their imprisonment to get money for drugs. Drug-related homicides in the United States average around 17,000 per year. More than 40 percent of violent crimes committed against college students including rape and sexual assault are committed by drug users. The most used drugs in the United States are marijuana, cocaine, heroin, opiates, depressants, and stimulants.[17]

America's drug problem has been exacerbated by the disaster at our southern border created in 2021 by the administration of President Joe Biden. Upon taking office in January 2021, President Biden opened the door to undocumented immigrants by eliminating most of the security measures his predecessor put in place to protect our southern border. The drug cartels seized on our now porous border as an opportunity to export even more drugs into the United States using illegal immigrants as drug mules and disguising drug pushers as immigrants seeking asylum in the United States.

America's "War on Drugs" was initiated during the Nixon presidency in the 1970s and achieved little or no success. Critics of the war on drugs claim it has failed miserably and should be replaced by: 1) legalizing drug use, and 2) establishing a broad-based program of treatment centers. We agree the War on Drugs as currently conducted is ineffective, but we disagree with legalizing drugs. Doing so might empty a lot of prisons but it will not eliminate the human costs of drug abuse.

What You Can Do about the Drug Cartels

One of the first things that must be done to decrease the size of the drug problem in America is decreasing the demand for drugs. We speak to how this can be done in chapter 2 (the "hub") of this book: "Achieving an American Spiritual Revival." Young people who learn to look to God through Jesus Christ for comfort, solace, and reassurance when life gets hard do not need to seek those things in drugs. Consequently, your first step in solving the drug cartel problem in America is doing your part to bring about the spiritual revival explained in chapter 2. But a spiritual revival will take time and persistence. In the meantime, a new approach is needed for combating the drug cartels.

As president, Donald Trump raised the issue of designating drug cartels as foreign terrorist organizations (FTOs). Although he had the support of some members of Congress, the idea was dropped when opponents of this approach pointed out drug cartels do not meet the criteria for FTOs set forth in Title 8 U.S. Code 1189 because their motives are profit-driven rather than ideological. Opponents claim because of this drug cartels must be treated like criminal organizations rather than terrorist groups.

Opponents of the FTO designation miss an obvious point. Their argument simply points to a weakness in the law rather than a weakness in the proposed designation. Congress makes the laws and Congress can revise them. Drug cartels kill more Americans with their illegal products each year than terrorists. It is not likely Americans affected by these deaths are overly concerned about hairsplitting distinctions concerning motives.

We recommend Congress revise Title 8 U.S. Code 1189 to allow violent drug cartels to be classified as FTOs. This will allow the cartels to be eliminated using covert Special Operations teams in the same way terrorist leaders and groups are eliminated. Since the cartels doing the most damage in the United States are in Mexico, the president and defense department will have to covertly liaison with that country's leadership and Mexican Marines and Special Ops Forces to implement this strategy. This takedown and its planning must be a very closely held. We know many of Mexican leaders/politicians are compromised by the cartel leadership. In fact, joint special operations missions involving both countries are doable with trusted entities.

Just as the "War on Terrorism" is misnamed, so is the "War on Drugs." The former is a war on terrorists not terrorism. The latter must be a war on drug cartels not drugs. If we are at war with drug cartels, we should proceed accordingly. Our Special Operations troops have the capabilities required to eliminate existing drug cartels and make the formation of new ones too expensive and too deadly to contemplate. All that is needed is the political will in Washington, DC.

This is where you and other American patriots come in. Your role in this endeavor is to: 1) encourage Congress to revise Title 8 U.S. Code 1189 to allow drug cartels, 2) encourage the president and state department to undertake the necessary negotiations with Mexico and other South and Central American countries, 3) encourage the president, as commander in chief, to instruct the Pentagon and the US Special Operations Command to develop an operational plan to neutralize and destroy the cartels.

Here is the plan we recommend. Begin with unconventional/conventional war planning. This approach combines the best use of special operations teams, drones, and air assets encompassing intelligence, targeting, base operations, offensive and defensive operations, and structural organization of our forces to accomplish the mission. Task the Special Operations Command (SOCOM) to build and develop a war plan to locate and neutralize the five or six cartels operating out of northern Mexico. Task the Treasury Department with tracking the international banking accounts of the cartels and affiliates and stop the flow of money.

SOCOM should use existing bases (lily pads) in the border states to launch operations (e.g., Fort Hood and Fort Bliss, Texas, Fort Huachuca, Arizona, and Camp Pendleton, California. There is no need to create new bases. Locate selected units and personnel at these designated bases. Work with Mexican officials to establish a twenty-mile "control zone" on the Mexican side of the border. Any group or individuals occupying this zone and engaged in criminal or illegal activities against Mexico or the United States will be engaged on sight.

The mission for the command structure is to target and conduct offensive and defensive operations on the Mexican side of the border. National Guard, Border Patrol, DEA, and local sheriff's units will conduct border security operations on the United States side of the border. This initiative does not violate any existing Posse Comitatus laws. A cohesive, well-thought-out plan such as this can neutralize the cartels in seven days.

Congress must feel the pressure of the American people to solve the drug and sex trafficking conducted and supported by the cartels and stop the illegal migrant invasion of America.

NEW CALIPHATE IN AFGHANISTAN

For Americans, the war in Afghanistan began in 2001 in response to Al-Qaeda's 9/11 terrorist attacks masterminded by Osama Bin Laden which killed 3,000 people. Following the attacks, Bin Laden took refuge in Afghanistan under the protection of the Taliban. When the Taliban refused to hand over Bin Laden, the United States intervened militarily.

The war in Afghanistan finally came to an ignominious end when President Joe Biden ordered a precipitous evacuation of all American troops from the country. The United States surrendered in Afghanistan! Biden's feckless, incompetent handling of the evacuation created a humanitarian disaster for the Afghan people and Americans who were unable to get out. It also left the country in the hands of the Taliban, sworn enemies of the United States. With free reign over the country, the Taliban wasted no time in proclaiming the establishment of a new caliphate in Afghanistan.

A caliphate is a government ruled by a caliph, an Islamic spiritual leader in line of succession from the prophet Muhammad. A caliphate is a theocracy ruled according to Islamic law. What this means to America is after twenty years of fighting in Afghanistan to prevent terrorist attacks on the United States, that country will become a haven where terrorist groups—including Al-Qaeda—can plot such attacks. Afghanistan, in the aftermath of President Biden's disastrous surrender, will become a launching pad for jihadists attacks on "the Great Satan," the name given to America by radical Islamic terrorists. They likely now include the pejorative "coward" to describe us thanks to the Biden regime.

What You Can Do about the New Caliphate in Afghanistan

Before getting into what you can do about the new caliphate in Afghanistan, we summarize what the United States must do. Your job as a patriot wanting to save America is to support the following strategies:

- Continue efforts overt and covert to bring home Americans who remain stranded in Afghanistan. Every American remaining in Afghanistan is a potential victim for Taliban blackmail.
- Charge the CIA with the difficult task of finding ways to rebuild a network on the ground for monitoring events in Afghanistan.
- Refuse to normalize relations with the Taliban. Its leaders are starving for economic assistance and will promise anything to get it. America's leaders must not be misled by Taliban promises of moderation. They will never keep their promises.
- Support Ahmad Massoud and other credible resistance leaders. When the people of Afghanistan have suffered enough under the Taliban's harsh rule, they will turn to resistance leaders like Massoud. A civil war against the Taliban could be in Afghanistan's future.
- Use every means—diplomatic, economic, and military—to prevent Afghanistan from becoming an Al-Qaeda stronghold and to minimize China's influence on that country. If necessary, implement the Lily Pad strategy to neutralize Al-Qaeda/ ISIS operatives and potential training bases in Afghanistan.

As is the case with several of the foreign and domestic threats to America's end game for the twenty-first century, *your job as an American patriot is to pressure elected officials in Congress and the White House to do the right thing.* We believe the strategies recommended in this section are the right thing to do. Memorize them and be able to articulate them to elected officials and political candidates. Then support only those who will commit to these strategies.

UNCONVENTIONAL WARFARE: CYBER, BIOLOGICAL, VIRAL, AND SPACE

Because America's conventional and nuclear military capabilities are powerful deterrents to traditional attacks, adversarial nations such as The People's Republic of China (PRC) and Russia have developed alternative capabilities including cyber, biological/viral, and space warfare. The world got a mild preview of what a viral warfare attack might look like when the COVID-19 virus was spread from a laboratory in Wuhan, China.

Cyberwarfare is the use of computer technology to disable or disrupt operations of a government, military organization, or business. Cyberattacks can take several forms including data breaches, account hijacking, extortion, data manipulation, misconfiguration, and operational shut-downs. The greatest cyberwarfare threats to the United States come from Russian and China. Russia used cyberattacks to interfere in the presidential election of 2020 in which Joe Biden was named president.

The United States has powerful cyberwarfare capabilities including offensive, defensive, and intelligence-gathering potential. The National Cybersecurity and Communication Intelligence Center, a component of the Department of Homeland Security (DHS), is America's nerve center for responding to cyberattacks. As advanced as the DHS capabilities are, the United States is still vulnerable to cyberwarfare, particularly America's private sector.

A particularly attractive target for cyberattacks is the nation's critical infrastructure grid. For example, ransomware attacks in 2021 on the Colonial Pipeline and Steamship Authority of Massachusetts. Infrastructure interruptions result in shortages, increased costs of goods and services, and financial loss due to operational shutdowns and ransom demands paid.[18]

Biological and viral warfare represent deadly threats to America's end game for the twenty-first century. The COVID-19 pandemic of 2020, 2021, 2022, and its residual impact reveals how vulnerable the United States is to this unconventional form of attack. The COVID-19 virus was spread from a laboratory in Wuhan, China. The CCP denies this accusation, but it always denies its nefarious schemes. A possible explanation for the COVID-19 pandemic is it was an intentional act on the part of the Chinese Communists to evaluate the efficacy of biological and viral warfare. It is well known the Chinese military has an advanced biological warfare program that includes research, development, production, and weaponization capabilities. The PRC has a variety of delivery systems for its biological and viral weapons including artillery, rockets, aerial bombs, sprayers, and ballistic missiles.

Writing for *Health Express*, a part of Observer Research Foundation, Javin Aryan stated:

> . . . a document recently came to light that has reinvigorated the origin debate (of COVID-19) and brought the research and development of biological weapons back into focus. Titled, *The Unnatural Origins of SARS and New Man-Made Viruses as Genetic Bioweapons*, the paper was written in 2015 by 18 Chinese military scientists and weapons experts. They stated that a family of viruses called coronaviruses could be 'artificially manipulated into an emerging human disease virus, then weaponized and unleashed in a way never seen before.'[19]

In 2019, the world began to feel the effects of the COVID-19 pandemic.

The Center for Health Security at the Johns Hopkins Bloomberg School of Public Health summarizes the threats faced by our country as follows:

> In terms of deliberate threats, we continue to face the prospect of biological weapons attacks, both from known very high consequence pathogens, such as the agents that cause anthrax and smallpox, as well as unknown novel and engineered biological threats. Epidemics could also emanate

from pathogens that are released from research labs accidently, including from laboratories working on non-circulating viruses such as SARS or smallpox, or from research work that has created novel epidemic strains of pathogens.[20]

The largest biological and viral threats to the United States come from Russia, China, North Korea, and Iran. However, any country with life-science capabilities can sequence and synthesize biological and viral components turning them into lethal weapons. One can now go online and learn how to engineer deadly biological and viral pathogens. As a result, new threats can be developed faster than defenses against them.[21]

For decades, the United States had a decided advantage over all adversaries in space warfare capabilities. This is the good news. The bad news is our military has become dependent on satellite communication and GPS in conducting operations. This dependence makes us vulnerable to countries developing technologies to destroy satellites. Both Russia and China now have these satellite-destroying technologies. In addition, both countries have invested heavily in offensive space weapons. Iran and North Korea, though not yet as advanced as Russia or China, are moving in that direction.

China has organized its space warfare forces under a new major force structure responsible for space, electronic, and cyberwarfare. The Communist Chinese have launched a new space plane like the U.S. Air Force's X-37B space plane, a smaller fully-robotic version of the space shuttle. The CCP's SJ-17 satellite can maneuver near other satellites and conduct proximity operations and surveillance. The PRC is in the process of developing a space station that should be operational no later than 2024. The first module of the space station was launched by a Long March 5B rocket in May 2021. It is also developing a heavy-lift rocket, the Long March 9, and a second space launch vehicle, the 921 rocket. The 921 rockets will be able to conduct circum-lunar missions. Finally, the PRC is developing ground-based directed-energy weapons able to disable satellites.[22]

The changing situation in the space warfare arena is why Congress and President Donald Trump established a new arm of the U.S. military: U.S. Space Force and Space Command. America's new Space Force is focused on developing and deploying offensive and defensive space warfare capabilities.

What You Can Do about Cyber, Biological, Viral, and Space Warfare

As is the case with most of the foreign threats to America's end game for the twenty-first century, your job is to understand what the government and Department of Defense must do to overcome the threats and to encourage elected officials to do what is necessary to safeguard America's future. Here are the strategies we recommend in this vital area of national interest:

- Strengthen the National Cybersecurity and Communication Intelligence Center by giving it the resources to attract and retain the best and brightest in this field. Task the Center with working closely with the private sector to harden its system against cyberattacks. Make grants available to assist selected universities in developing state-of-the-art degree programs in cybersecurity. Also make grants—not loans—available to high scoring students on a competitive basis who wish to pursue careers in cybersecurity. Make enhanced cybersecurity a high priority in government, the military, and critical sectors of the private economy.
- There is no way to prevent rogue nations from developing biological and viral weapons if they have a life-science capability. Engineering biological and viral weapons is not difficult for scientifically capable nations. Therefore, the United States must implement two strategies at once. First, use the hard lessons learned from the COVID-19 pandemic to prepare the nation's medical infrastructure to respond quickly, efficiently, and effectively to an attack. Make sure the medical equipment, drugs, and supplies are in place and ready to access at a moment's notice. Also make sure frontline medical personnel have been trained to respond. Second, let the world know any biological or viral attack on the United States will be considered an act of war and will result in a swift and deadly response. Our government

officials should make it known to the world no military option is off the table should biological or viral weapons attack us.

- To overcome space warfare threats, the United States must fully develop, properly fund, and uncompromisingly support the new Space Force. Just as our military has historically established itself as the world's leader on the ground, in the air, on the sea, and under the sea, we must now establish ourselves as the unquestioned leader in space.

A patriot who wants to save America and ensure a bright future for our country is to encourage and force elected officials in the strongest terms to implement the strategies recommended herein. Here is where your voice can be effective. Overcoming these unconventional warfare threats as well as all foreign threats to our future will be expensive.

Therefore, elected officials must re-orient their priorities and stop wasting money needed for our national defense on hyper-expensive social programs that turn American citizens into entitled, dependent, helpless wards of the state. All the social spending in the world will be of no avail if we fail to do what is necessary to protect the American people from the foreign threats explained in this chapter.

INTERNATIONAL SHADOW GOVERNMENT/FIFTH COLUMN

Who really runs the world? Is it the elected and unelected heads of state who are known to the world, or is it powerful men and women who pull their strings from behind a curtain of secrecy? Is there an international shadow government or fifth column of influential people who are the puppet masters for the heads of state? To answer these questions, it is necessary to know about the Bilderberg Group, an organization comprised of bankers, oligarchs, tech czars, politicians, and business tycoons.

The Bilderberg Group meets annually and is attended by 120 to 150 government, business, industrial, academic, finance, and media leaders from Europe and North America. The meetings are convened in Europe and North America giving attendees opportunities to discuss common problems, ideas, and strategies. Following each meeting a private report is circulated to participants—past and present—with speakers identified by country but not name.[23]

Participants in the Bilderberg Group have a high level of influence in their respective nations and use it to influence democratic elections.

Because of the influence of people on Leftist politicians such as Barack Obama and Joe Biden, the Bilderberg Group represents a clear and present danger to the United States, a nation that is supposed to be a government of, by, and for the people.

What You Can Do about the Global Shadow Government

The solution to the fifth column the global shadow government represents is complete transparency. American patriots who want to save our country from those who would destroy it must understand the concept of government by the governed and insist elected officials and political candidates confront the members of the Bilderberg Group and demand transparency. Government officials from our country should collaborate with their counterparts in other countries to apply appropriate pressure on the Bilderberg Group to open its meetings to the public, publish minutes of all meetings, and subject themselves to media scrutiny.

EPILOGUE

A GREAT AWAKENING: A PICTURE OF AMERICA WHEN OUR COUNTRY IS SAVED

America's Endgame for the 21st Century contains a blueprint for defeating the Leftist ideologues who are trying to transform the United States into a Marxist "paradise" like other socialist states around the globe that have failed miserably and sacrificed millions of lives. The blueprint also covers how to overcome specific domestic and foreign threats to our nation's sovereignty and survival. Saving America from the Left as well as the domestic and foreign threats we have identified in this book is a challenge of monumental proportions. It will require American patriots to join in a united front, stand up, speak out, and be counted. Fortunately, this is beginning to happen even as we write these words. It is critical that the global, one world, elitists be neutralized. We do not need any "shadow groups, cabals, or shadow governments to replace our patriotic, national governments functioning under the Constitution as written.

In 2021, with Joe Biden in the White House and the extreme socialist wing of the Democrat Party controlling him and the Party, Leftist ideologues who had been using the "boiling the frog" strategy since the 1960s shifted their efforts into high gear. Here is a brief overview of what these anti-American ideologues did in 2021 in pursuit of their Leftist agenda:

167

- Implemented a COVID-19 vaccine mandate robbing individual Americans of their right to have a say in their own healthcare decisions
- Told parents they had no say in their children's education
- Encouraged large cities across the country to defund their police departments
- Sided with rioters who burned and looted cities and attacked law enforcement officers and law-abiding citizens
- Paid American citizens to sit idly at home rather than working, thereby creating a major workforce shortage that drove many small businesses out of business
- Taught Critical Race Theory (CRT) to young school children against the express wishes of their parents and labelled parents who complained "domestic terrorists"
- Forced military personnel to sit through absurd Leftist indoctrination courses teaching the lie that white people are perpetual oppressors and minorities are perpetual victims
- Lobbied to force white people who never owned slaves to pay reparations to black people who were never slaves
- Changed the focus of the military from being prepared to defend our country from foreign enemies and terrorists to an obsession with so-called "social justice" issues. Badly needed training dollars were diverted to counterproductive uses such as providing sex-change operations for transgendered troops.
- Browbeat athletic associations into allowing transgender men to compete against biological women
- Encouraged schools to allow transgender boys to use girl's bathrooms and then tried to cover up the predictable problems when they occurred

In addition to these strategies of the far Left, there are several other concerns that cannot be overlooked as patriots move forward to save our country from the radical ideologues trying to destroy it. These concerns include the following:

- Fair and impartial elections are at risk because of Democrat chicanery. Evidence continues to pile up to suggest the 2016 presidential election was rife with fraud. For example, Democrats, including President Barack Obama and candidate Hillary Clinton, loudly and persistently accused Donald Trump of colluding with the Russians to steal the election. We now know, just the opposite happened. The Russian collusion story was a hoax perpetrated by Democrats in an attempt to steal the election from Trump. Special counsel John Durham's investigation into the Russia collusion story prove it was a hoax perpetrated by Hillary Clinton's campaign. In November 2021, Durham began issuing indictments. For example, in the first week of November, Igor Danchenko, a Russian national working for the Brookings Institution in Washington, DC was indicted and named as the main source for the Christopher Steele dossier. This false dossier was the basis for the allegations against Donald Trump. Also implicated by Durham's investigation was Clinton associate and public relations executive, Charles Dolan.

- Another concern relating to fair and impartial elections is outside interference in the form of cyberattacks. Serious questions have been raised concerning Russian and Chinese interference in the 2020 presidential election in key battleground states including Arizona, Nevada, Wisconsin, Michigan, Pennsylvania, and Georgia. Putting the claims and denials aside, the one irrefutable fact in this case is the Russians and the Chinese have both the motive and the ability to use cyberattacks to alter the outcome of presidential and Congressional elections in America. Therefore, hardening our electoral systems against cyberattacks and our citizens from corrupt media influence must be a priority for patriots who want to save America.

- Biological attacks on the United States—particularly from the People's Republic of China (PRC)—must be treated as a real threat. No one in the Biden administration wants to discuss the possibility, but based on statements on the record by People's Liberation Army General Chi Haotian, the COVID-19 pandemic could have been a deliberate test by the People's Liberation Army (PLA). According to General Chi Haotian, biological warfare is a fundamental part of the PRC's warfare doctrine. The origins of the COVID-19 pandemic and the motive of those behind it must be investigated, nailed down, and responded to appropriately. The danger of another even more dangerous virus being released on the world—perhaps in time to impact the 2022 mid-term elections—is a distinct possibility based on the comments of the Chinese general.

- The Biden administration is pursuing policies that weaken the United States, undermine its credibility on the world stage, threaten our economy, and move our country closer every day to becoming a socialist dystopia, which is just one step from communism. His tax-and-spend policies coupled with his allegiance to the "Green New Deal" have already caused massive inflation and are moving the country toward hyper-inflation. Biden's unconscionable handling of the Afghanistan surrender undermined America's credibility on the world stage, gave the People's Republic of China (PRC) an edge in southwest Asia, and encouraged terrorists worldwide. Support of Leftist ideologues in the Democrat Party for the Marxist Black Lives Matter movement and defunding the police caused a major spike in violent crime in major American cities while also signaling open season on law-abiding citizens to criminals. By putting their imprimatur on racially-divisive concepts such as Critical Race Theory and the 1619 Project, Biden and the Leftist ideologues who control him put an end to E Pluribus Unum, replacing it with racial strife and on-going contention.

- The influence of a shadow government over the Biden administration and American politics in general must be a serious concern for patriots who want to save America. This topic was discussed in chapter 8. We raise the issue again here to emphasize its importance. It is especially important to determine what role Barack Obama and the Clintons play in this shadow government and how much influence they are exerting on key Biden staffers left over from the Obama administration. These staffers include Susan Rice, Jake Sullivan, and Ron Klein. Is Joe Biden president of the United States or just a puppet whose strings are pulled by the extreme Left of the Democrat Party? Patriots who want to save America must answer this question.

- In summary, a cold war with the Chinese Communists has already started, a cold war that could lead to World War III. The Biden administration is complicit through negligence, incompetence, and an "anything China wants China gets" policy in bringing this dangerous situation about.

With their puppet in the White House and control of Congress in their hands but sensing they might lose control of Congress because of their anti-America agenda, the Left tried to reshape America in its own distorted image prior to the 2022 mid-term congressional elections. This turned out to be a bridge too far for a lot of Americans. Patriotic Americans who believe in freedom, individual liberty, and the other values that have historically defined our country finally began to say, "enough is enough." America's Great Awakening had begun.

AMERICA'S GREAT AWAKENING

In 2021, hundreds of thousands of American citizens refused to take the mandated COVID-19 vaccination even though doing so cost them their jobs and even careers. Highly-trained military personnel well into their careers said "no" to the vaccine mandate as did several cadets at West Point. Doctors, nurses, truck drivers, civilian defense contractors, and other critical personnel walked off their jobs rather than submit to government coercion over the COVID-19 vaccine.

At a time when businesses throughout the country were struggling to attract and retain enough employees to keep their doors open, hospitals were crying out for nurses and doctors, and a shortage of truck drivers was creating bare shelves in grocery stores, the far-Left regime of President Biden was forcing in demand, highly skilled personnel who refused the vaccination to either quit or be fired from their jobs. Americans of all political persuasions began to say, "enough is enough."

As Leftist governors, mayors, and city councils in many of America's large cities defunded their police departments, forcing law enforcement officers by the thousands to retire, resign, or be fired, violent crime in their cities skyrocketed. Understandably, citizens and business owners began to flee these out-of-control cities for safer territory. Finally, the remaining citizens said, "enough is enough." Leftist elected officials were forced to begin re-funding their police departments. Many of these Leftist ideologues masquerading as city officials were voted out of office in November 2021.

Parents who objected to their children being taught Critical Race theory (CRT) and other Leftist tripe began attending school board meetings and making their voices heard. When they were told by school board members and teachers' union officials they had no say in what their children were taught, their numbers increased as did the volume of their voices. When concerned parents were labelled "domestic terrorists" for speaking out on behalf of their children, they finally said "enough is enough."

America's Great Awakening began to reveal itself in tangible terms when in the off-year elections of 2021, Leftist candidates were turned out of office in droves. The best example of this phenomenon was the gubernatorial race in Virginia, one of the bluest of the blue states in America. Democrats controlled the state's government for decades until conservative American patriots who believed in the vision of the Founders and the rights of parents turned out in unprecedented numbers to defeat the Democrat candidates for governor, lieutenant governor, and attorney general. They also took control of the Virginia House of Delegates. America's Great Awakening portends badly for far-Left Democrats in the 2022 mid-term elections.

To continue what has begun because of America's Great Awakening, patriots from across the country must come together and do the hard work of fully implementing the blueprint for saving America set forth in this book. We must achieve an American Gospel revival, preserve the Constitution and Bill of Rights, reject historical revisionism, refute the big lies of the Left, reject socialism, preserve capitalism, restore patriotism, and love of country, and overcome the domestic and foreign threats that can keep us from achieving America's end game for the twenty-first century.

When we complete all the steps in the blueprint set forth in this book our republic will be saved. What will that look like? Our

Founders answered this question for us when they drafted the Constitution. They eloquently painted a beautiful picture of their vision for America in the Preamble to our Constitution:

> We the people of the United States, in Order to form a more perfect Union, establish Justice, insure domestic Tranquility, provide for the common defense, promote the general welfare, and secure the blessings of Liberty to ourselves and our Posterity, do ordain and establish this Constitution for the United States of America.

When patriots come together and completely implement the blueprint set forth in this book for rescuing America from the Leftist ideologues bent on destroying our country, we will have that "more perfect union" the Founders envisioned. There will be equal justice for all American citizens, domestic tranquility instead of violent riots, the strongest, best-equipped, best-trained, best-led military in the world on land, in space, on the sea, in the air, and under the sea, a high quality of life for all citizens based on personal responsibility and initiative, and freedom and liberty for ourselves, our children, and our posterity throughout successive generations.

All American patriots have an important role to play in saving our country from those who want to destroy it. If we band together with saving America as our common goal, we will achieve America's end game for the twenty-first century and, as a result, re-establish that "more perfect union" envisioned by our Founders. Together, we can make it happen. Let us get started. Thanks be to God for his mercy upon which we call and depend for the salvation of America.

AUTHOR BIOGRAPHIES

Lt. General Thomas McInerney. January 2000, Lieutenant General Thomas McInerney, USAF (Ret.), established his own consulting firm, GRTT (Government Reform Through Technology). Working with high-tech companies who do business with federal, state, city and local governments, GRRT helped them introduce advanced technology into the public sector. He has since shifted his activities to Purpose Built Edge Clouds.

From March 1996 to December 1999, he was Chief Executive Officer and President of Business Executives for National Security (BENS), a national, nonpartisan organization of business and professional leaders, with headquarters in Washington, DC. BENS works to engage the business community in securing America's future with a more efficient defense establishment. In February 2000, General McInerney received a Laurel from Aviation Week and Space Technology magazine for his efforts on behalf of military reform as president of BENS. He has also made numerous appearances on national television discussing defense reform and global military crises such as Kosovo, EP 3 incident in China, and now the War on Terrorism where he was the senior Fox News Military Analysts from 2001–2017.

Prior to joining BENS, General McInerney was Vice President of Command and Control for Loral Defense Systems-Eagan. He joined Loral (then Unisys Electronic Systems Division) in 1994 following thirty-five years as a pilot, commander, and Joint Force Commander in the United States Air Force.

General McInerney retired from military service as Assistant Vice Chief of Staff of the Air Force and as director of the Defense Performance Review (DPR), reporting to the Secretary of Defense.

In that capacity, he led the Pentagon's "reinventing government" effort, visiting more than 100 leading-edge commercial companies to assimilate their ideas about business re-engineering. The DPR was part of Vice President Gore's National Performance Review on Reinventing Government, which focused on making the government perform better at less cost—a fundamental BENS objective.

After his commissioning as a second lieutenant in 1959, and completion of pilot training in 1960, General McInerney served in numerous key Air Force assignments and had extensive military command and overseas experience. A command pilot with more than 4,500 flying hours, he completed four tours of duty in Vietnam, flight reconnaissance missions during the Cuban missile crisis, and air escort missions in the Berlin Corridor. He commanded a Major Air Command, two Numbered Air Forces, an Air Division and a Tactical Fighter Wing as well as a Category 3 Test Team introducing two new fighter aircraft into combat in Vietnam.

General McInerney earned a Bachelor of Science degree from the U.S. Military Academy in 1959 and a master's degree in international relations from George Washington University in 1972. He completed Armed Forces Staff College in 1970 and the National War College in 1973.

In 2011 General McInerney helped form YottaStor a Cloud Computing LLC with emphasis on Large Object Data Storage especially for Intelligence, Surveillance and Reconnaissance (ISR) platforms as well as Medical Imaging, Agriculture Imaging, Disaster Recovery, Continuity of Operations Planning (DR/COP), and recently during CV 19 Administrative Oversight and Compliance.

MG Paul E. Vallely was born in DuBois, Pennsylvania, and served a distinguished career of thirty-one years in the U.S. Army before he retired as Deputy Commanding General, U.S. Army Pacific, in Honolulu, Hawaii in 1992. General Vallely graduated from the U.S. Military Academy at West Point and earned his commission in the Army in 1961.

General Vallely is a graduate of the Infantry School, Ranger and Airborne Schools, Jumpmaster School, the Command and General Staff School, the Industrial College of the Armed Forces, and the

Army War College. His combat service in Vietnam included positions as infantry company commander, intelligence officer, operations officer, military advisor, and aide-de-camp. He has over fifteen (15) years' experience in Special Operations, Psychological Operations, and Civil-Military Operations.

After serving in two combat tours in Vietnam, he also served in several other overseas theaters in Europe and Pacific Rim countries. Vallely served on U.S. security assistance missions and on civilian-military relations tours in Europe, Japan, Korea, Thailand, Syria, Iraq, Kuwait, Turkey, Israel, Indonesia, and Central America. He has served as a consultant to the Commanding General of the Special Operations Command as well as the DOD Anti-Drug and Counter-Terrorism Task Forces. He also designed and developed the Host-Nation Support Program in the Pacific for the DOD and the State Department.

MG Vallely has been on radio and television for many years, most notably serving as the senior military analyst for the Fox News Channel from 2001–2008. He is a guest lecturer on multiple issues including national security, international politics, economics, strategic planning, U.S. foreign policy, and the Global War against Radical Islam, and other threats to America. He and LTG Thomas McInerney co-authored the book *Endgame: Blueprint for Victory for Winning the War* on Terror. MG Vallely conducts an average of four-to six national radio/TV show interviews per week and is well known for his published articles and talks on National Security and domestic issues.

Vallely is the Founder of Nemo Arms Inc. of Boise, Idaho, and is the Chairman of Stand Up America US Foundation. He also chairs the Legacy National Security Advisory Group and is a founding member of the Citizens Commission on National Security. He led fact-finding missions into Syria with his team, once traveling deep inside the Syrian war zone to Aleppo. Additionally, during that period, he co-chaired two separate delegations to Cairo, Egypt, to meet with President El-Sisi and his senior staff. Most recently, he was invited to Europe and Russia to present his six-point plan for solving the European/Syrian Refugee crisis. Most recently, he launched his own radio show, *The Stand Up America US Show*.

Paul and his wife, Marian, reside in Montana. Both are deeply involved in numerous humanitarian efforts and are active participants in a multitude of community events and activities.

Dr. David L. Goetsch is a Marine veteran and author of seventy-eight books, several of which are best sellers. Eight of his books have been translated into foreign languages including Indonesian, Korean, Malaysian, Spanish, Hindi, and Turkish. Dr. Goetsch is a long-time college professor with dual credentials in business and political science/history. He is also a nationally recognized speaker on the subject of leadership.

He holds an associate degree, bachelor's degree, four master degrees, and a doctorate. In 2016, Dr. Goetsch was inducted into the Florida Veteran's Hall of Fame for his military service and contributions to the state of Florida in the areas of economic development, higher education, and civic leadership. He is also a member of his community's Civic Leaders Hall of Fame.

Dr. Goetsch holds numerous awards including the "Spirit of Freedom Award" from Freedom Newspapers and the George Washington Medal of Freedom awarded by the Freedoms Foundation at Valley Forge. He was the founding chairman of the Florida Defense Support Task Force where he worked with then Governor Rick Scott and the Florida Legislature to help make Florida the most military-friendly and veteran-friendly state in the U.S.

NOTES

CHAPTER 1: A BLUEPRINT FOR SAVING OUR COUNTRY

1. *Ashcroft v. The Free Speech Coalition*, 535 U.S. 234 (2002), Retrieved from http//:www.casebriefs.com/blog/law/constitutional-law/constitutional-law-keyed-to-cohen/restrictions-on-time-place-or-matter-of-expression/Ashcroft-v-the-free-speech-coalition-/ on September 19, 2021.

2. Gillespie Shields, "Forty Facts About Two Parent Families," Retrieved from https://gillespieshields.com/40-facts-two-parent-families/ on September 20, 2021.

3. SAVE: Suicide Awareness Voices of Education, Retrieved from *Suicide Statistics and Facts—SAVE* April 1, 2022.

4. Military Enlistment Oath, Retrieved from https://www.military.com/join-armed-forces/swearing-in-for-military-service.html on September 21, 2021.

5. National Archives, "The Constitution of the United States: A Transcription," Retrieved from https://www.archives.gov/founding-docs/constitution-transcript on September 15, 2021.

6. Gary Alder, "A Paraphrase of Federalist No. 39," Retrieved from https://www.freedomformula.us/articles/federalist-39-paraphrase on September 29, 2021.

CHAPTER 2: ACHIEVING AN AMERICAN SPIRITUAL REVIVAL

1. As quoted in "America Needs Revival" by Greg Laurie. Retrieved from https://thinke.org/blog/does-america-need-a-revival-by-greg-laurie .html on September 23, 2021.

2. Laurie, "America Needs Revival."

3. Angela Cleary, "Why We Need a Spiritual Revival Today More Than Ever," Retrieved from https://resoundinghislove.com/spiritual-revival/ on September 23, 2021.

4. Sy Miller and Jill Jackson, "Let There Be Peace on Earth," Retrieved from https://thepreachersword.com/2015/12/08/peace-on-earth-begins-with-me on September 24, 2021.

5. Gregory Elder, "Professing Faith: The religious foundations that bolstered the Declaration of Independence," July 24, 2019, Retrieved from https://www.redlandsdailyfacts.com/2019/07/04/professing-faith-the-religious-foundations-that-bolstered-the-declaration-of-independence/ on September 24, 2021.

6. Daniel Dreisbach, "'The Mythical 'Wall of Separation': How a Misused Metaphor Changed Church-State Law, Policy, and Discourse," June 23, 2006, Retrieved https://www.heritage.org/political-process/report/the-mythical-wall-separation-how-misused-metaphor-changed-church-state-law on September 24, 2021.

7. National Archives, "Declaration of Independence: A Transcription," Retrieved from https://www.archives.gov/founding-docs/declaration-transcript on September 24, 2021.

8. National Archives, "The Constitution of the United States: A Transcription," Retrieved from https://www.archives.gov/founding-docs/constitution-transcript on September 27, 2021.

CHAPTER 3: PRESERVING THE CONSTITUTION AND BILL OF RIGHTS

1. National Archives, "Declaration of Independence: A Transcription," Retrieved from https://www.archives.gov/founding-docs/declaration-transcript on September 28, 2021.

2. Abraham Lincoln, "The Gettysburg Address," Retrieved from www .abrahamlincolnonline.org/lincoln/speeches/gettysburg.htm on September 28, 2021.

3.   Edward S. Greenburg and Benjamin I. Page, *America's Democratic Republic*, 3rd Edition (New York: Longman, Pearson, 2009), 31–32.

4.   National Archives, "The Constitution of the United States: A Transcription," Retrieved from https://archives.gov/founding-docs/constitution-transcript on September 28, 2021.

5.   Nicolas Loris and Katie Tubb, "4 Reasons Trump Was Right to Pull Out of the Paris Agreement," Heritage Institute, Retrieved from https://www.heritage.org/environment/commentary/4-reasons-trump-was-right-pull-out-the-paris-agreement on September 28, 2021.

6.   National Archives. "The Constitution of the United States: A Transcription," Retrieved from https://archives.gov/founding-docs-/constitution-transcript on September 29, 2021.

7.   Jeremy Rabkin, "The Constitution and American Sovereignty," Imprimis, Retrieved from https://imprimis.hillsdale.edu/the-constitution-and-american-sovereignty/ on September 29, 2021.

8.   James Madison, "From James Madison to Henry Lee, 25 June 1824," Retrieved from https://founders.archives.gov/documents/Madison/04-03-02-0333 on September 29, 2021.

9.   Mark Levin, *Liberty and Tyranny: A Conservative Manifesto* (New York: Threshold Editions, 2009), 40.

10. National Archives, "Declaration of Independence: A Transcription," Retrieved from https://www.archives.gov/founding-docs/declaration-transcript on September 29, 2021.

11. National Archives, "The Constitution of the United States: A Transcription," Retrieved from https://archives.gov/founding-docs/constitution-transcript on September 29, 2021.

12. Stephen Flick, "The Godless Constitution?" Retrieved from https://christianheritagefellowship.com/the-godless-constitution/ on September 29, 2021.

CHAPTER 4: REJECTING HISTORICAL REVISIONISM AND REFUTING THE LIES OF THE SECULAR LEFT

1.   *Everson v. Board of Education of the Township of Ewing*, Retrieved from https://www.oyez.org/cases/1940-1955/330us1 on October 4, 2021.

2.   *Engle v. Vitale*, Retrieved from www.oyez.org/cases/1961/468 on October 4, 2021.

3. *School District of Abington Township, Pennsylvania v. Schempp*. Retrieved from www.oyez.org/cases/1962/142 on October 4, 2021.

4. Zachary Faria, "The Left is trying to redefine critical race theory because it's losing," *Washington Examiner*, June 16, 2021, Retrieved from https://www.yahoo.com/now/Left-trying-redefine-critical-race-174600042.html on October 4, 2021.

5. Timothy Sandefur, "The 1619 Project: An Autopsy," October 27, 2020, Retrieved from https://www.cato.org/commentary/1619-project-autopsy on October 5, 2021.

6. Sandefur, "The 1619 Project."

7. Kathryn Watson and Grace Segers, CBS New Report, September 18, 2020, "Trump blasts 1619 Project on the role of Black Americans and proposes his own 1776 Commission," Retrieved from https://www.cbsnews.com/news/trump-1619-project-1776-commission/ on October 5, 2021.

8. Jewish Virtual Library, "Joseph Goebbels: On the Big Lie," Retrieved from https://www.jewishvirtuallibrary.org/joseph-goebbels-on-the-quot-big-lie-quot on October 6, 2021.

9. "Joseph Goebbels."

10. "Joseph Goebbels."

11. Robert Morgan, "The Prayer That Saved the Constitution," February 5, 2020, Retrieved from https://faithgateway.com/the-prayer-that-saved-the-constitution/#.YWA59hrMKUK on October 8, 2021.

12. George Washington's Mount Vernon, "Thanksgiving Proclamation of 1789," Retrieved from https://www.mountvernon.org/education/primary-sources-2/article/thanksgiving-proclamation-of-1789/ on October 8, 2021.

13. Founders Online, "From John Adams to Massachusetts Militia, 11 October 1798," Retrieved from https://founders.archives.gov/documents/Adams/99-02-02-3102 on October 8, 2021.

14. Plimoth Patuxet Museums, "Mayflower and Mayflower Compact," Retrieved from plimoth.org/for-students/homework-help/mayflower-and-mayflower-compact on October 8, 2021.

15. G. Q. Pan, "North Carolina County to Discipline, Fire Teachers Who Say America and Founders Are Racist," *The Epoch Times*, October 3, 2021, https://www.theepochtimes.com/mkt_app/north-carolina-county-to-discipline-fire-teachers-who-say-america-and-founders-are-racist_4029554.html.

CHAPTER 5: PRESERVING CAPITALISM—REJECTING SOCIALISM

1. Oliver L. North and David L. Goetsch, *We Didn't Fight for Socialism: America's Veterans Speak Out* (Nashville: Fidelis Publishing, 2021), iii.
2. Walter Williams, "America's immorality will bring this nation down," *Northwest Florida Daily News*, April 2, 2009.
3. Max Weber, *The Protestant Ethic and the Spirit of Capitalism* (1905), 17.
4. Study.com: Puritan Work Ethic: Definition & Overview—Video & Lesson Transcript | Study.com Retrieved April 1, 2022.
5. George Bernard Shaw, "Forbes Quotes," Retrieved from https://www.forbes.com/quotes/3418/ on October 11, 2021.
6. Gallup: Socialism, Capitalism Ratings in U.S. Unchanged Retrieved from https://news.gallup.com/poll/357755/socialism-capitalism-ratings-unchanged.aspx March 31, 2022
7. Eberle, "Socialism vs. Capitalism."
8. Eberle, "Socialism vs. Capitalism."
9. Oliver North and David L. Goetsch, *We Didn't Fight for Socialism— America's Veterans Speak Up* (Nashville: Fidelis Publishing, 2021), 194.
10. David Lamb, *Vietnam, Now: A Reporter Returns* (Cambridge, MA: PublicAffairs, a member of the Perseus Group, 2002), 70.
11. Lamb, *Vietnam, Now.*

CHAPTER 6: RESTORING PATRIOTISM AND LOVE OF COUNTRY

1. Marc Thiessen, "Disrespecting the flag is a disgraceful way to protest Trump," *Washington Post*, September 25, 2017, https://www.washingtonpost.com/opinions/disrespecting-the-flag-is-a-disgraceful-way-to-protest-trump/2017/09/25/506a1d4c-a228-11e7-b14f-f41773cd5a14_story.html.
2. Edward Sutelan, "Hope Solo says Megan Rapinoe would 'almost bully' players to kneel during anthem; Solo left USWNT in 2016," Retrieved from https://www.sportingnews.com/us/soccer/news/hope-solo-megan-rapinoe-kneel-uswnt-2016/iqwe8q931zh415gaj0pfaj90c on October 14, 2021.
3. Armstrong Williams, "The NFL's decision to play 'Lift Every Voice and Sing' is a false start," *The Hill*, July 30, 2021, Retrieved from https://

thehill.com/opinion/civil-rights/564859-the-nfls-decision-to-play-lift-every-voice-and-sing-is-a-false-start on October 14, 2021.

4. Walter Sharp, "What percentage of NFL players are black," Retrieved from https://www.sportsskeeda.com/nfl/what-percent-nfl-players-black on October 15, 2021.

5. Williams, "The NFL's decision to play 'Lift Every Voice and Sing' is a false start."

6. Jeffrey Mirel, "The Decline of Civic Education," *Daedalus* 141, no. 2, 2002.

7. Adam Kirsch, "American Patriotism Is Worth Fighting For," *Wall Street Journal*, October 18, 2019, Retrieved from https://www.wsj.com/articles/american-patriotism-is-worth-fighting-for-11571413398 on October 18, 2021.

CHAPTER 7: OVERCOMING DOMESTIC THREATS TO THE END GAME

1. Clyde Wayne Crews Jr., "How Many Rules and Regulations Do Federal Agencies Issue?" August 15, 2017, Retrieved from https://www.forbes.com/sites/waynecrews/2017/08/15/how-many-rules-and-regulations-do-federal-agencies-issue/#74e122f11e64 on October 20, 2021.

2. Crews, "How Many Rules and Regulations Do Federal Agencies Issue?"

3. LegBranch Team, "How Many Congressional Staff Are There?" June 20, 2016, Retrieved from https://www.legbranch.org/2016-6-17-how-many-congressional-staff-are-there/ on October 21, 2021.

4. Mark Pullum, "The Quandary of Judicial Review, "*National Review*, April 8, 2015.

5. Chris Edwards, "A Plan to Cut Spending and Balance the Federal Budget," June 23, 2017, Retrieved from https://www.downsizinggovernment.org/plan-to-cut-federal-spending on October 21, 2021.

6. Edwards, "A Plan to Cut Spending."

7. VeryWellMind: "What Is a Sense of Entitlement?" Retrieved from https://www.verywellmind.com/what-is-a-sense-of-entitlement-5120616 on March 31, 2022.

8. Vladimir Lenin, Goodreads, Retrieved from https://www.goodreads.com/quotes/6825820-the-capitalists-will-sell-ys-the-rope-with-which-we on October 22, 2021.

9. Lee Rosebush, "Outsourcing Drug Manufacturing to China Was a Mistake—A Lethal One," *Newsweek*, May 5, 2020,Retrieved from https://www.newsweek.com/pharmaceutical-manufacturing-america-china-lethal-mistake-1502008 on October 22, 2021.

10. Irwin M. Stelzer, "Lenin Was Right," *Washington Examiner*, April 24, 2015, Retrieved from washingtonexaminer.com/weekly-standard/Lenin-was-right on October 22, 2021.

11. Meredith McGraw, Tina Nguyen, and Cristiano Lima, "Team Trump quietly launches new social media platform," July 1, 2021, Retrieved from https://www.politico.com/news/2021/07/01/gettr-trump-social-media-platform-497606 on October 22, 2021.

12. Major Cities Chiefs Association, Intelligence Commanders Group. "Report on the 2020 Protests and Civil Unrest," Retrieved from https://majorcitieschiefs.com/wp-content/uploads/2021/01/MCCA-Report-on-the-2020-Protest-and-Civil-Unrest.pdf on October 25, 2021, p. 7.

13. "Report on the 2020 Protests and Civil Unrest," 11.

14. "Report on the 2020 Protests and Civil Unrest," 13.

15. "Report on the 2020 Protests and Civil Unrest," 23.

16. "Report on the 2020 Protests and Civil Unrest," 26.

17. National Police Support Fund, "What Happens When Cities Defund Police Departments," March 4, 2021, Retrieved from https://nationalpolicesupportfund.com/what-happens-when-cities-defund-police-departments/ on October 25, 2021.

18. Victor Davis Hanson, "What Happened to the Beloved Military?" October 21, 2021, Retrieved from https://www.realclearpolitics.com/2021/10/21/what_happened_to_the_beloved_military_554328.html on October 25, 2021.

19. Hanson, "What Happened to the Beloved Military?"

20. Petr Svab, "Wokeism Undermining Operation of Military, Army Officer Says," October 12, 2021, Retrieved from https://www.theepochtimes.com/wokeism-undermining-operation-of-military-rmy-officer-says_4045412.html on October 25, 2021.

21. Hanson, "What Happened to the Beloved Military?"

22. Eileen Sullivan and Miriam Jordan, "Illegal Border Crossings, Driven by Pandemic and Natural Disasters, Soar to Record High," Retrieved from https://www.nytimes.com/2021/10/22/us/politics/border-crossings-immigration-record-high-html on October 25, 2021.

23.   Ira Mehlman, "40,000 COVID-Infected Migrants Released into the U.S. as the Nation Braces for Next Wave of the Pandemic," Retrieved from https://www.fairus.org/border-security/40000-covid-infected-migrants-released-us-nation-braces-next-wave-pandemic on October 25, 2021.

24.   Mehlman "40,000 COVID-Infected Migrants Released."

25.   Paul E. Vallely, "US Border Plan to Secure America," Stand Up America US Foundation, March 26, 2021, Retrieved from https://standup americaus.org/us-border-security-plan-and-the-cartels/ on October 25, 2021.

26.   Vallely, "US Border Plan to Secure America."

27.   Idaho, Office of the Governor, "Joint Policy Framework on the Border Crisis," October 26, 2021, Retrieved from gov.idaho.gov/presdrelease/governors-detail-their-policy-solutions-to-alleviate-border-crisis/ on October 25, 2021.

CHAPTER 8: OVERCOMING FOREIGN THREATS TO THE END GAME

1.   The Policy Planning Staff, Office of the Secretary of State, "The Elements of the China Challenge," November 2020, (Revised in December 2020), Retrieved from state.gov/wp-content/uploads/2020/11/20-02832-Elements-of-China-Challenge-508.pdf on October 27, 2021, p. 4.

2.   "The Elements of the China Challenge," 8–16.

3.   "The Elements of the China Challenge," 8.

4.   "The Elements of the China Challenge," 10.

5.   "The Elements of the China Challenge," 13.

6.   Robert O. Work and Greg Grant, "Beating the Americans at Their Own Game: An Offset Strategy with Chinese Characteristics," June 6, 2019, Retrieved from https://www.cnas.org/publications/reports/beating-the-americans-at-their-own-game on October 27, 2021, pp. 5–6.

7.   "The Elements of the China Challenge," 46–50.

8.   "The Elements of the China Challenge," 3.

9.   Alexis Mrachek, "Assessing Threats to U.S. Vital Interests," The Heritage Foundation, Retrieved from https://www.heritage.org/military-strength/assessing-threats-us-vital-interests/russia, on October 28, 2021.

10.   Mrachek, "Assessing Threats to U.S. Vital Interests."

11.   Mrachek, "Assessing Threats to U.S. Vital Interests."

12. ADL, "The Iranian Nuclear Threat: Why It Matters," Retrieved from https://www.adl.org/resources/fact-sheets/the-iranian-nuclear-threat-why-it-matters on October 28, 2021.

13. United States Department of State, Bureau of Counterterrorism, "Country Reports on Terrorism: Iran," Retrieved from https://www.state.gov/reports/country-reports-on-terrorism-2019/Iran/ on October 28, 2021.

14. Paul E. Vallely, (Major General, U.S. Army, retired), Legacy National Security Advisory Group, "Joint Operations Task Force," PowerPoint presentation provide by the author.

15. Vallely, "Joint Operations Task Force."

16. U.S. Department of Justice, "Drug Trafficking Organizations," Retrieved from https://justice.gov/archive/ndic/pubs38/38661/dtos.htm on October 29, 2021.

17. Bureau of Justice Statistics, "Drug Use and Crime," Retrieved from https://bjs.ojp.gov/drugs-and-crime-facts/drug-use-and-crime on October 29, 2021.

18. "The 10 Biggest Ransomware Attacks of 2021," November 12, 2021, https://illinois.touro.edu/news/the-10-biggest-ransomware-attacks-of-2021.php.

19. Javin Aryan, "A look at China's biowarfare ambitions," June 2, 2021, Retrieved from https://www.orfonline.org/expert-speak/a-look-at-chinas-biowarfare-ambitions/ on November 3, 2021.

20. Johns Hopkins, Bloomberg School of Public Health, Center for Health Security, "Biological Threats to US National Security," Retrieved from https://www.centerforhealthsecurity.org/our-work/publications/biological-threats-to-us-national-security on November 1, 2021.

21. "Biological Threats to US National Security."

22. Mandy Mayfield, "China's Ambitious Space Programs Raise Red Flags," July 2, 2021, Retrieved from nationaldefensemagazine.org/articles/2021/7/2/chinas-ambitious-space-programs-raise-red-flags on November 3, 2021.

23. Ed Haugland, "Ruling Global Elites (A Global Shadow Government) Buy and Steal America," Retrieved from https://www.govinfo.gov/content/pkg/CHRG-112shrg72480/html/CHRG-112shrg72480.htm on November 3, 2021.